Television Segmentation
How the American Model was Exported to Brazil

Luiz Guilherme Duarte, Ph.D.

www.vide-u.com

DEDICATION

A man, and his work for such matter,
is the sum of his experiences. This work is dedicated to my wife and family, who gave me some
of my most significant experiences.

ACKNOWLEDGMENTS

All those who so friendly gave of their wisdom and at-
tention, with special appreciation to professors: Joseph
Straubhaar, Thomas Baldwin, Gilbert Williams, José
Marques de Mello, and Sebastião Squirra.

TABLE OF CONTENTS

Tables

Figures

Preface

W hat was the single most important marketing trend in the television business in the last decade of the 20th Century? Most of the dozens of professionals interviewed for this book seem to agree that segmentation was the keyword for any study on the television scenario. The purpose of this study, conducted in the early 1990s and still relevant as a historical document, is to review the development of television segmentation in the United States and its influence in the Brazilian industry, which was only recently going through a segmentation process.

Many Business Administration researchers have long identified a general tendency of companies to move the focus of their operations from inside themselves toward their customers. In the past, production and selling techniques, allied with product innovations, were the key to success, but the long-term satisfaction of customers has become more important in modern times. It is the so-called "Marketing Concept" that works for television just as well as it does for any other industry. The concept's premise is that the organization that identifies the needs/wants of a target segment of the total consumer population and satisfies that segment more efficiently than its competitors is more likely to succeed. One of the world's leading authorities on marketing, American economist Philip Kotler, laid the theoretical basis for this trend in the 1980s. He described how "mass marketing" had been replaced by a more efficient "target marketing," in which the companies segment the total set of consumers to better attend to a specific group of them.

Kotler's work can be considered a benchmark to which most studies on market segmentation relate, and it is repeatedly quoted throughout this study as a source of enlightenment to the business data presented. Building on Kotler's theories, advertising men Al Ries and Jack Trout have proposed some practical tactics to conquer a position in the marketplace, which are applied to the American and

1

Brazilian television industries in Chapter 1. As this study indicates, these industries have gone through the same evolutionary process just described, starting with a mass audience and focusing their efforts on target segments of the public, as competition increased, as publics changed and as new signal distribution technologies were made available.

In Chapter 2, the original mass medium is revisited, highlighting the close resemblance of the two national industries. The brief historical review of television's early days was based on the perspective of the marketing studies conducted by Brazilian scholar Cesar Bolaño and was summarized only to provide a better understanding of present developments. Since the Brazilian environment (in social, economic and business terms) is significantly different from the American one, a tendency to follow the American example has apparently been balanced with adaptations to Brazilian laws, policies, and reduced audience acquisitive power.

In the 1980s, the regular broadcasting networks had their mass market swept away and started to segment the market among themselves. Chapter 3 describes how new networks have appeared in both countries with successful marketing strategies that target smaller—but high consumption groups, which are very attractive to advertisers. Most of the ever present relevance of this television segmentation study comes from the creation, in the late1980s, of new channels in Brazil, based on a variety of contemporaneous signal distribution technologies, including open ultra-high frequency (UHF) channels, subscription TV (STV), multipoint multichannel distribution systems (MMDS), direct broadcast satellite (DBS) and cable. The UHF seemed to be Brazil's priority at the time and, as the initial focus of this study, deserved a more detailed analysis.

The subject of Chapter 4 is the introduction of these systems in Brazil and United States, indicating the problems and pitfalls the American entrepreneurs have found which may serve as guidelines for the Brazilian experiences. After all, access to and the use of a certain technology constitutes a form of segmenting the market as well. Another form of television segmentation is based on programming variations, and Chapter 5 describes the profile of the new Brazilian companies and their programming lineups, most of them imported at the time. The global flow of programs had changed a lot in the last decade of the 20th Century, however, and the imported schedules were expected to be replaced over time by more international co-productions. For the existing Brazilian audience of the new channels at the time, on the other hand, the production effort may not be necessary.

As Chapter 6 discusses, these new channels are mostly reaching the upper classes, which demand more internationalized programming and are probably happy with the early imported programming lineups. Moreover, such elitism denoted an audience segmentation based on social class, rather than on taste or important demographics, as it happens in the United States. Overall, this study documents an important transition phase in Brazilian television. It concludes that Brazilian television has followed the American industry in the past and now has the chance to make up for the delay in adopting new technologies and segmentation marketing. Despite the significant economic difficulties faced by the Brazilian entrepreneurs, the prospective profits are high, and the new systems were likely to increase their base to include the middle classes and more local productions.

Luiz Guilherme Duarte

1
Television Segmentation

In the communication jungle out there, the only hope to score big is to be selective, to concentrate on narrow targets, to practice segmentation. In a word, "positioning" (Ries & Trout, 1981, p.6).

Broadcasting. As the name suggests, television was, once, defined simply as a medium designed to reach a broad or wide audience by casting its message in all directions. In America, as well as in Brazil—the two countries analyzed in this study—the costs were paid by advertisers, and every TV set owner within a station's coverage area could freely receive the signals. In fact, as Browne reminds us:

> As advertising costs are passed along to the consumer in the price of the product or service, obviously the audience does pay. But presumably not all of the audience pays equally, and certainly the audience is less aware of paying for broadcasting in this way than it is with annual license fees or individual contributions (Browne, 1989, p.18).

Under this perspective, it has been said that television's product for sale is not its programs, but its viewers. Broadcasters sell their ability to reach the audiences to the advertisers, who pay the production of programming that will attract the public. To ensure that their money is well spent, advertisers want to reach as many viewers as possible. Or, using the advertising jargon, they want to have the lowest CPM (cost per thousand) viewer in every spot aired. Adopting Philip Kotler's terminology, it was the "mass marketing" era. Author of "Principles of Marketing," one of the bibles of business administration, Kotler characterizes this seller as a "mass-producer, mass distributor, and mass-promoter of one product to all buyers" (Kotler, 1986). In other words, broadcasters filled their schedules with very few program formulas distributed in a network basis to one mass of audience (the real product). Usually, individual consumers become masses when there is

5

an excess demand and, in this case the audience wanted television as much as the advertisers wanted the audience. Both market demands (for television and for audience) are further identified along this study, according to Kotler's parameters:

> Market demand for a product is the total volume that would be bought by a defined customer group in a defined geographical area in a defined time period in a defined marketing environment under a defined marketing program (Kotler, 1986, p.247).

Television programming and its respective audiences in the Unites States and Brazil are analyzed with special attention to the demographic, economic, technological, political and cultural environment in which the companies develop their strategies. For now, it is sufficient to say that the dropping prices of mass-produced TV sets and the novelty of a "radio with images" attracted an excess of public and advertising demand in the early days of television (50s and 60s). Companies would advertise anything, even specialty products of very restricted interest, while viewers would tolerate long sequences of commercials. Without recognizing the similarity to early American TV, a BusinessWeek article of 1967 comments:

> The advertisers are pleased with the Brazilian audience tolerance for long parades of commercials and announce everything, including even heavy machineries ...; audience acceptance of programming— any programming—is so whole-hearted that there appears to be little need to strive for perfection (1967).

In both countries, television was born with a private nature and supported by the dual demand of advertisers and audience. In this early phase, entire programs could be purchased, with the sponsor playing a major part in the mechanics of production. And, since viewers were not very critical about TV, little concern was placed on knowing the audience demands. With a few years of experience, however, the audience learned to be more selective, and broadcasters' competition soon brought to an end the so-called "anything-goes" years that lasted until the early and late 1960s in America and Brazil, respectively. The decline of non-critical viewership and the rising expectations of audiences were first identified by the Bower Report, which compared studies conducted in 1960 and 1970. The report's conclusions indicated that, even though people were watching and enjoying more TV, their enthusiasm for it had vanished. It had become more socially desirable to be against television, and survey respondents' answers showed that they would rather criticize the low-brow programming than confess their viewership. Illustratively, 70 percent of the 1970 respondents agreed that there were too many commercials, compared to 75 percent that in 1960 agreed commercials were a fair price to pay for entertainment. At that point, the successful programming formulas of the past were copied by new entrants—the me-too companies—but new programming formulas also caught on, diversifying viewers. The Bower Report specifically mentions that "TV had ceased to be primarily an entertainment center and had become a major force in journalism as well" (Bower, 1973).

A "product-differentiated marketing"—a typical business concept that implies a range of operational tactics, according to the various lines of products—was introduced. And television became not only a source of entertainment, but also of information and education, attracting more and different viewers. Audience tuning started to be more carefully surveyed and differentiated according to programming preferences. Still in search of the largest possible share of the market, the regular surveys started to dictate the success of programming in terms of prices for advertisements—"spots." And, even though new programming formulas were adopted to offer variety, television broadcasts were still trying to be everything for everyone. For the old pioneers of this industry, like American NBC or Brazilian Globo, megalomania (I would call it "Lincoln's Test"[1]) may even be harmless. But new players, who still have to win the competition to prove their own right for existence, certainly cannot afford it. In the words of Ries and Trout:

> Today, the everybody trap may keep you afloat if you ... already own a substantial share of market. But it's deadly if you want to build a position from nowhere (Ries & Trout, 1981, p.76).

Ries and Trout's theory is that the media battle for the audience's

---

1 The test is to prove whether Abraham Lincoln's famous phrase—"You can fool all of the people some of the time, some of the people all of the time, but you can't fool all of the people all of the time."—was right or wrong.

attention (mind) had reached a saturation point. There are so many messages "bombarding" the individuals in the viewing audience that they are not capable of assimilating most of the messages made available. Individuals are bombarded not only from television, but from newspapers, magazines, radio, billboards, conversations, etc. The assimilation screening process, they say, tends to select oversimplified messages informing about things one knows nothing about (first impression) or confirming things already known (familiar). Thus, since the screening process is so dramatic, they defend that one should "concentrate on the perceptions of the prospect (audience). Not the reality of the product." Translating the theory to the television industry, programmers should concentrate their efforts on that small fraction of messages that is assimilated by a specific group of the audience instead of offering all kinds of programming for all groups within the audience. Indeed, MTV's revolutionary programming (the first impression) or AMC's old movies (the familiar) are examples of successful strategies to win out in the audience's screening process.

In the early 1980s, when these two advertising men infuriated their colleagues with their no-nonsense ideas about the new marketing challenges, television had become a much more complex industry than it was in the early days. Television broadcasting revealed itself as limited in its initial concept. The narrow frequency band assigned in the over-the-air radio spectrum restricted the number of stations, the few programming schedules did not attend to all public demands; hence, those too distant from a station were simply deprived of television. Using new kinds of signal distribution technologies, the development of other concepts of television gradually solved most of these problems in America. More bands of the spectrum were transferred to television services, increasing coverage and allowing for the creation of paid channels watched by subscribers only. Cable systems ended the finite spectrum discourse offering more than thirty channels of varied programming and satellite relays put everyone at the reach of television. By the end of the 20th Century, all of these new technologies allowed, for example, the coexistence of seven VHF (very high frequency) and eight UHF (ultra high frequency) stations in New York City, besides 17 basic cable channels and seven premium services. The multitude of options, however, made Lincoln's Test practically unbeatable. It is still possible to attract some viewers, some time, but not everyone all the time. Competition is much harder when the audience has to choose among four dozen channels. Ries and Trout explain that:

> We have become an overcommunicated society ... Our extravagant use of communication to solve a host of business and social problems has so jammed our channels that only a tiny fraction of all messages actually get through. And not the most important ones either (Ries & Trout, 1981, p.11).

Ries and Trout's "positioning" concept matches Kotler's suggestion that "today's companies are moving away from mass marketing and product-differentiated marketing toward target marketing" in which the "seller distinguishes between market segments, selects one or more and develops programs and marketing mixes tailored to each one." As he puts it:

> Organizations recognize that they cannot appeal to all buyers in the markets, or at least not to all buyers in the same way. The buyers are too numerous, widely scattered, and varied in requirements and buying [viewing] practices. ... Instead of scattering their marketing effort ('shotgun' approach), they can focus it on buyers who have the greatest purchase interest ('rifle' approach) (Kotler, 1986, p.262).

Thus, while the broadcasting networks lose audiences for their mass appeal programs, the new cable networks have been carving out a significant corner of the market by tailoring programs to specific segments of the market (See Table 1). About 90 million households watched the American networks in the beginning of the 1980s. After only ten years, this number fell to 64 million, a loss of 29 percent of the market (See Figure 1) (1991t). Most of the lost audience was lured away by cable television, which conquered 24 percent of the market in the same period (See Figure 2). And, with the audience shift, the revenues also shifted from one system to another. Cable consultant Paul Kagan estimated that the revenues of the American cable industry increased almost twenty times in the last decade of the century (See Figure 3). Comparatively, cable advertising was still a fraction of broadcasters' and subscriber fees remained the main financial source of the industry. In 1990, advertisers invested about $1.4 million on cable, against $9.4 billion on the broadcast networks (Monush, 1992).

Table 1 - The 20 largest American cable networks

Network	Focus	Subscribers (000)
1. ESPN	Sports	54,000
2. CNN	News	53,200
3. Nickelodeon	Children	50,000
4. MTV	Music (12-34 years)	49,900
5. Nashville	Country Music	49,000
6. Discovery	Education	46,800
7. Lifetime	Women	46,000
8. The Weather Channel	Temperature, weather	41,000
9. Headline News	News	40,400
10. A&E	Arts, shows	36,000
11. VH-1	Music (25-45 years)	35,900
12. Financial News	Economy, business	32,000
13. Black Entertainment	Music, black culture	26,000
14. Learning Channel	Education	18,000
15. Travel Channel	Travel information	15,000
16. Consumer News (CNBC)	Shopping, economy	14,000
17. Sports America	Sports	8,500
18. Nostalgia	Over 45 years old	8,000
19. The Comedy Channel	Comedy	6,000
20. Galavision	Latin public	2,000

Source: Cable TV Facts 90. By Cable Television Advertising Bureau, Inc.

Nevertheless, companies had been increasingly attracted by the highly qualified cable TV audience, which presents a higher education and income, being more likely to consume in quantity and better (See Table 2). To understand the value of a qualified audience to advertising supported media, it is interesting to see how a media expert in an advertising agency works.Usually, when faced with the task of selecting the best medium or group of media to carry the client's message, the advertising professional asks two simple questions: Who is the consumer of the product?

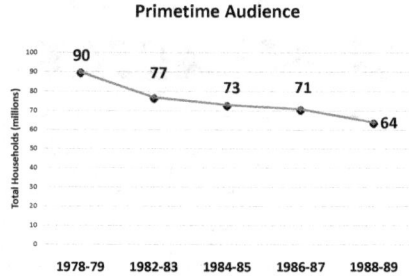

Figure 1 - American broadcasting networks lose audience

Source: Cable TV Facts 90. By Cable Television Advertising Bureau. Inc.

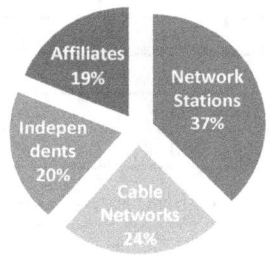

Figure 2 - American cable channels won 24% of audience

Source: Cable TV Facts 90. By Cable Television Advertising Bureau. Inc.

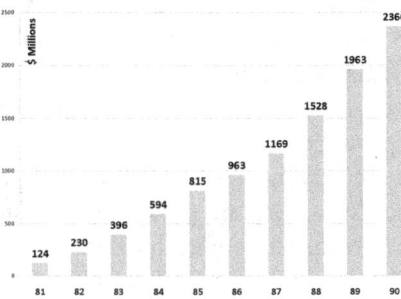

Figure 3 - American cable revenues rose 20 times in a decade

Source: Paul Kagan Associates, Inc. in Cable TV Facts 90. By Cable Television Advertising Bureau. Inc.

11

Table 2 - American cable audience is upscale

	USA	Cable	Big Three
Annual Family Income			
Above $60,000	100	125	96
$40,000 -$60,000	100	115	99
$20,000 -$40,000	100	104	101
Below $20,000	100	72	101
Education			
College Graduate	100	113	102
Attended College	100	114	97
HS Graduate	100	103	102
Not HS Graduate	100	78	99
Occupation			
Executive	100	130	99
Professional	100	108	98
Other employed	100	99	96

Source: Cable TV Facts 90. By Cable Television Advertising Bureau. Inc.

What media are more likely to reach this consumer with the minimum waste? Thus, instead of television, a financial newspaper like The Wall Street Journal is probably a better medium for the advertising of a new, complex financial calculator. Among the hundreds or millions of television viewers, only a few would be interested or could afford the calculator and the investment would be dispersed. On the other hand, most of the Wall Street readers constitute prospective consumers of this product and the focusing pays off. If the product were mainly consumed by housewives, like a liquid detergent, the situation is reversed. Matching the product's consumer profile to the media's audience characteristics may look like a simple exercise of common sense, but there are various theories behind it. Overall, the theories indicate that advertising is more effective when targeted at individuals whose problems or needs can be solved by the product. In the book Consumer Behavior, Schiffman and Kanuk explain that:

Marketers do not create needs, though in some instances they make consumers more keenly aware of unfelt needs. Successful marketers define their markets [and their media] in terms of the needs they are trying to satisfy, rather than in terms of the products they sell (Schiffman & Kanuk, 1991, p.68).

In the past, each and every medium was a mass medium. There were fewer important newspapers, magazines, radio and television stations competing in the market, and all of them enjoyed large readership/viewership. So the media professionals would choose the medium for an advertising campaign according to its intrinsic characteristics and the demands of the product: radio favored services and other conceptual products instead of visual ones, television was better able to demonstrate the use of the product, and the printed medium's advantage was its permanent character; details could be listed that consumers could consult whenever desired. But as advertisement waste became a concern, each medium was subdivided according to identifiable market segments. Today, there are hundreds of magazines segmented by readers' interest (cars, computers, sailing, etc.), newspapers segmented by geographical focus (local, state, national), and FM radio stations segmented by music genres (rock, classic, country, etc.). Television followed this trend more recently, with ethnic channels and, later, cable networks focused on cartoons, movies, news, music, etc. The segmentation has allowed advertisers to reduce wasting efforts by reaching more people than the ones that may actually consume the products. Segmentation was the key to the coexistence of many more players in the market, a fact that is only possible because they do not necessarily compete for the same theoretical consumer/audience.

Instead of going after a small share of a large market, which would hardly be enough to support their expensive operations, the American cable networks pursued a large share of a small market. According to Kotler, they practice "concentrated marketing." Their greater knowledge of the segment's needs bring economies of specialization in production, distribution and promotion. Hence, while Nickelodeon cable network may be the best choice to advertise products for children, ESPN is more suitable to sports merchandise, and so on. The risks, warns Kotler, are the entrance of strong competitors or the possibility

13

that segment may turn "sour." The Comedy Channel and Ra, for example, competed in the comedy segment until the market proved to be too small for two companies, and they were forced to merge. The avoidance or reduction of risks requires a careful segmentation analysis that takes into consideration the size and profitability of the market (substantiality)—assuming they can be measured (measurability)—to design programs (actionability) to reach these people (accessibility). The segments are then defined by combining geographic, demographic, psychographic and behavioristic variables. In the United States, age (demographic) variables, for instance, can be recognized as one of the most important variables in marketing segmentation. Researchers have identified that consumers between 18 and 40 years old, followed by teenagers, are the ones with the most money and willingness to consume.

In the television industry, this explains why advertisers pay more for shows that have this audience, even though the ratings may be lower (Zoglin, 1990). Today, the advertising demand is for a quality audience, not quantity anymore. A show once had to attract about 30 percent of the total viewers to be considered a success. But as the audience got more fragmented, a program can stay alive if it is watched by as little as 21 percent of the audience[2] (Sanoff, 1985). And this fight for quality audience instead of mass audience is not restricted to segmented channels. The broadcasting networks were once said to have lost the qualified audience to the new technologies, keeping only the masses who cannot afford other systems and who are uninteresting to the advertisers. Nevertheless, broadcasting networks too have looked for the audience that can bring more advertising dollars.

The new Fox broadcasting network has conquered audience and advertisers, programming exactly for the economically attractive younger public. As cable television reached 60.3 percent of American TV homes in 1991, the broadcasting networks remain the only option for many people, but significant changes have been undergone in the Big Three—NBC, CBS, and ABC (Monush, 1992). Still operating in several segments of the market, the Big Three have designed separate programming offers for each segment, "hoping for greater repeat viewership because the offer matches the demand rather than the other

---

2 This figure has proven to be lower and lower over time.

way around." The practice of Kotler's "differentiated marketing" can strengthen viewers' overall identification of the channel with the programming, the most important element in conquering the audience. A 1983 article at Atlantic magazine explained "why the networks will survive cable":

> The way the programs reach the audience or the quantity of signals reaching it is not as important as the quality of the programming. Without different ideas for programming to fill the new channels, even the new technologies will be in trouble. And if the programming on the paid systems is not really different from the free TV, the networks win (Mink, 1983).

The strategy, however, brings an inevitable increase in the cost of doing business (more production, administration and promotion expenses), which the broadcasters have coped with in many different ways. At first, the networks tried to combat cable by offering similar programming, especially movies. In 1985, a record 110 original made-for-TV movies were scheduled by the networks (Sanoff, 1985). The expenses were high and the results were very poor until the networks realized that cable's weakness was actually their high reliance on movies. The same Atlantic article explains:

> There are not enough good movies to be shown and they are forced to repeat the same movie many times. Even different channels play the same movies around the same period. Subscribers are frustrated and cancel the pay channels ... To distinguish from one another, pay channels are producing movie-like programs, cheaper than theatrical features, but more expensive than made-for-TV. But the more unknown productions they add, the harder it is for the viewer to differentiate them from the free programs produced by the networks (Mink, 1983).

Another adaptation has been to look for ways to reduce programming costs. One of the most praised programs of the time was "America's Funniest Videos," which portrays viewers' amateur video productions with little or no cost to the network. Reality shows, like "Cops" and co-productions with overseas broadcasters are also examples of cheaper productions. More commonly, networks started airing more live programming and series that air more than once a week (Zoglin, 1990). However, while management is still trying to invent ways of reducing the cost of what they are doing, a sharp distinction between the networks is still hardly discernible. Except by Fox's strategy to go after the baby-boomer, this author's foreign eyes failed to recognize a more elaborate segmentation among the broadcasting networks. In sports, for example, they have had difficulties competing for programming with cable's deep pockets. The 1992 Olympic Games transmission on a Triplecast pay-per-view basis by NBC was considered a sign that the network acknowledged the higher profitability of cable systems. If asked, most Americans would probably identify the networks in terms of their local newscast or situation comedies (sitcoms), and a scholar could as well define the networks' market niche in terms of these program formulas.

1.1 Will Brazil follow the American example?

"We may assume from the start that no two broadcast systems are absolutely alike," said Browne in the introduction of his book, comparing broadcast systems (Browne, 1989). But it is precisely from the similarities to the American experiences that this study tries to extract some benchmarks for the analysis of the segmentation trend in Brazilian television. Only eight years separate the initial commercial operations of television stations in the United States and Brazil. Since then, the South American country has closely followed the development of the North American television industry. Most of Brazil's equipment and programming have been imported from the United States and an agreement with Time-Life even brought to Brazil the American management system.

The developmental phases are also comparable. Most scholars in both countries recognize how television, born an elite's toy, quickly conquered the masses, technologically expanding to trespass national borders. In "Um Perfil da TV Brasileira," Sergio Mattos describes four phases in the Brazilian television: the elitist (between 1950 and 1964), the populist phase (1964-1975), the technological development phase (19751985) and the transition and international expansion phase (1985-1990) (Mattos, 1990). Following the marketing analysis proposed before, this study suggests that after the elitist phase, in which only the elite had TV sets, came a mass marketing phase, in which Globo TV imported the American strategies and adapted them to a national version until the end of the military regime in the late 1970s.

With government support, the national telecommunications networks were strongly developed in this phase, and Globo's virtual monopoly allowed for the creation of a powerful national production center that now exports to more than a hundred countries around the world. The new Brazilian civil republic marked a third phase, one in which television's role as the regime's banner was softened by the creation of new networks and the appearance of some incipient alternative distribution systems. It is the present phase of market segmentation, where most networks positioned themselves around the programming strengths of the dominant network, TV Globo, using unconventional time slots to reach specific audience niches.

New players also entered the market, offering focused programming through additional advertising supported UHF (ultra high frequency) channels or pay-TV systems, like subscription television (STV), cable systems, multichannel multipoint distribution systems (MMDS) and direct satellite broadcasting (DBS). Several different factors had been leading Brazilian television toward target marketing. First, among the new entrants in the industry were old communication conglomerates, barred from television by the government, due to their traditional opposition standpoint. These groups had not only contributed with significant new capital, but had put their lobbying power to accelerate and concentrate a political basis for the regulation of new television services.

Comparatively, the new Brazilian TV entrants had been doing what cable operators did for American television, imposing the demands of the market over a government wary about multiplying media for opposing message makers. When comparing the United States with a Third World country, the economic inferiority of the latter is usually a major concern. But the delay of almost one decade for new signal distribution systems was more certainly caused by a government policy than by real economic difficulties. The approximate $1.4 billion that TV advertisements made in Brazil in 1989—about 70 percent of the national advertising investment—made Brazil the tenth largest advertising market in the world (1990h). This number was surpassed only by USA, Japan, United Kingdom, Italy, Spain, France, Germany, Australia and Canada. The Brazilian television profits were twice that of Colombia, which was ranked second in Latin America. And Brazilian profits were higher than the sum of profits in Portugal, Belgium, Greece and Netherlands (Hoineff, 1991). Moreover, if the economy were to be blamed for the delayed introduction of cable and other pay-TV systems, how would one explain the paradox that the debut of these systems occurred amidst one of the worst recessions that ever hit the country?

Second, the TV production technology available then in the international market had evolved to provide quality video at cheaper costs. The technology, as Chapter Four further argues, made it easier for Brazilian companies to produce their own programming or to buy them from local independent producers, which turns the fulfillment of more channels into a feasible and less expensive task. American television could not count on the same cheap and improved technology in the beginning of its segmentation drive, but the larger size of the U.S. market and their well developed cinema industry compensated for it. Many of the American segmented (cable) channels invested in the creation of new programming and networks, which presently provide the bulk of the schedule for the new Brazilian channels that long await the amortization of the initial investments to increase or start national production.

Third and most important, Brazilian advertisers had grown more interested in narrowing the target of commercials as the percentage of the population with significant acquisitive power had been consistently reduced in the last years due to the severe economic recession in the country. Thus, once again, Brazilian television seems to follow the trends of its American counterpart. The similarities and differences between the two experiences are going to be studied in the next chapters. Some elements are already expected to be revealed. The uneven distribution of the wealth in Brazil is likely to impede a significant absorption of expensive distribution technologies (pay-TV) by the society; at least at comparable levels. The network segmentation process also happens in an industry that is still practically monopolized by TV Globo, a nimble company capable of buying out any competitor's successful programming. The smaller size of the other television companies makes it difficult for them to produce quality programming and, if the target market is focused, the audience share may not initially payoff, requiring deep pockets or imported alternatives. Therefore, some of the questions to which this study tries to respond are whether there is a market to sustain cable, STV and DBS in Brazil; how the networks were positioning themselves; and how the new niche channels had imported or produced programs to attend to their specific audiences.

2
The Original Environment

The end of the product era came with an avalanche of me-too products that descended on the market (Ries & Trout, 1981, p.27).

Experimental operations of television stations in the United States date back to 1928, but the challenges to take television from the laboratories to the market were first faced by the initial ten commercial stations legally authorized to start operations on May 1942 (Yuster, 1992). In general marketing terms, the new-born industry followed its broadcasting predecessor—the radio—to implement strategies to increase consumers/advertisers' demand and to cope with the marketing environment. A new breed of professionals had to be recruited; since the TV device was new, additional accessory equipment had to be developed; while programs had to be created and produced to conquer audiences and advertisers. Along the years, broadcasters also had their business either restricted or boosted by government policies concerned with the value of the medium as a political tool and with a rather fuzzy "consumer interest, convenience and necessity." The Westinghouse company and other television manufacturers produced programs as a service to attract consumers.

The objective, Hoineff says, was to sell receivers to the audience and not the audience to the advertisers, which generated the concept of free programming (Hoineff, 1991). Nevertheless, television's marketing efforts to grow from an elite's toy to a real consumer product and a mass medium only gained impulse after 1952. Just six of the initial ten stations continued operations throughout World War II and, in 1948, new concessions were frozen due to the obvious incapacity of the very high frequency (VHF) waves to cover the whole country. There were about 108 stations in America then and, until the government decided upon new engineering standards and channel assignments, the industry was too fragile to pursue any long-term coherent marketing strategy. Thus, without disregarding the importance of these early experiences, it may be interesting to note that the Brazilian television industry has a business history almost as old as America's.

When newspaper entrepreneur Assis Chateaubriand opened the first station in São Paulo on September 18, 1950, he initiated an industry whose development across the years has closely resembled the American one. Similarly, both industries started with a private commercial nature a long time before any regulation had been conceived to determine their operation parameters. The first year of the pioneer TV station Tupi-Difusora was illustratively financed by four advertisers: Sul America (Insurance), Antarctica (Beverages), Laminação Pignatari (Metallurgy) and Moinho Santista (Food) (Mattos, 1990). Until approximately the mid-1950s, however, most Brazilian scholars (such as Caparelli and Mattos) seem to agree that television lived an experimental elitist phase as had happened in America before the war. According to Sergio Mattos, the main problem was difficult access to TV sets: "television was a luxury toy in its first two years. A TV set cost three times more than the most sophisticated radio available and just a little bit less than a car" (See Table 1). In the beginning, he says, there were fewer than 200 TV sets in the country, and Chateaubriand installed some sets in public parks to allow the general public to watch the programs. As depicted in the movie "Bye Bye Brasil," this practice remains common in some of the most distant and poor communities of the Northeast region of Brazil.

But the marketing environments were different and the Brazilian growth occurred in an accelerated time frame. In 1951 the production of TV sets in Brazil started with the Invictus brand, allowing a significant reception of the first soap opera in that same year ("Sua vida me pertence," by Walter Foster, from 12/21/51 to 2/15/52) (Fernandes, 1982). Instead of the depression of war that was experienced by the first American TV stations, Brazilians were living in a prosperous period, as the coffee farmers of São Paulo promoted industrialization and urbanism with their excellent revenues and the help of well-trained labor, represented by European immigrants.

A middle-class consumer market was in formation and the many American companies in Brazil knew, from their previous experiences in the United States, the value of television for advertising to this

Table 1 - Growth of TV set sales in Brazil

Year	B&W Sold	Color Sold	B&W+Color in Use
1951	3,500	-	3,500
1952	7,500	-	11,000
1953	10,000	-	21,000
1954	13,000	-	34,000
1955	40,000	-	74,000
1956	67,000	-	141,000
1957	81,000	-	222,000
1958	122,000	-	344,000
1959	90,000	-	434,000
1960	164,000	-	598,000
1961	200,000	-	763,00
1962	269,000	-	1,056,000
1965	370,000	-	1,993,000
1970	816,000	-	4,584,000
1972	1,109,000	68,000	6,250,000
1975	1,184,000	532,000	10,127,000
1979	1,591,000	1,074,000	16,737,000
1980	-	-	18,300,000
1986	-	-	26,500,000
1989	-	-	28,000,000

Source: Abinee (Associação Brasileira das Empresas de EletroEletrônica).

Reproduced from Bolaño, Cesar. Mercado Brasileiro de Televisão. Sergipe, UFS, 1988.

group. Through their advertising agencies, advertisers (especially the large multinational corporations) supported the production of programs for the mass audiences, besides the importation of American shows to fulfill schedules. A study of the Brazilian television market by Cesar Bolaño indicates that in 1952 TV Tupi/Difusora already surpassed the revenues of any radio station in São Paulo State and, in 1956, the total of television stations in São Paulo had revenues as high as the 13 largest radio stations in the State (Bolaño, 1988).

23

By the end of the 1950s, there were ten stations already in operation in Brazil and Chateaubriand's Diários Associados Group was the leader of the small oligopolistic industry. But while American TV drew most of its expertise from the powerful cinema industry, which also came to guarantee a steady provision of programming, Brazilian TV had to establish its own production centers. As the national cinema industry was dying under the American distributors' aggressive strategies, TV in Brazil grew under the influence of an already established radio industry, absorbing its structure, programming and even its professionals. The later consequences of this initial developmental difference will be commented upon in Chapter 5. Throughout the 1950s and 1960s, high production costs put American and Brazilian broadcasters in the hands of the advertisers, who determined the programs to be produced and transmitted, besides directly hiring artists and producers. Characteristically, the programs were identified by the sponsor's name, such as the famous "Repórter Esso," a news bulletin created in 1952 by Tupi/Rio station following the mode of another successful radio bulletin (Nogueira, 1988).

The reduction of the price of TV sets increased the penetration of television and the flow of advertising, allowing for the introduction of what many studies indicate as the first real mass-targeted service. TV Excelsior entered the market in 1960 with capital from Simonsen Group, which was connected to coffee exportation; it had the concession for Paranaguá Port and owned Panair Brasil. Excelsior imposed an aggressive strategy, stressing modern equipment and hiring the best professionals in the market with high salaries. Its programming strategy was based on two lines: the shows produced in Rio de Janeiro would attract the audience, and the soaps produced in São Paulo would retain that audience. Excelsior was also innovative by marketing its programming and artists as a differentiated product. In "Rio e Excelsior: Projetos Fracassados," Alcir Henrique da Costa states that Globo's programming and much of the present national programming formulas were first elaborated by Excelsior (Costa, 1986, p.123-66). Its parent company, however, faced difficulties under the post-1964 regime, and Excelsior lost financial support, closing in 1970. Brazilian expansion in this phase was more geographical than economical or corporative. The barriers to entry the industry were limited to the possibility of obtaining a concession to install a station, and at least one company in most major urban areas was granted a permit by the end of the 1960s. Significant difficulties to enter the television industry would only come later with Globo's virtual monopoly. As Litman explains:

> The greater the difficulty of new firms in entering an industry as significant competitive forces, the higher are the "barriers," and the greater the tendency for current firms to maintain high profit-maximizing prices with accompanying excess profits and misallocation of society's scarce resources (Litman, 1991, p.11).

Technological advancements and new legislation also favored the definitive establishment of mass television in Brazil. The Brazilian Telecommunications Code (CBT), approved by the National Congress on August 27, 1962, gave more guarantees to the stations and diminished prohibitions. It was an advance in the juridical definition of the concessions, keeping pace with technology developments, but it still reserved to the Executive the power to decide about the concessions. And in 1963, live television was regulated, while TV Rio and many other small stations had their survival assisted by the arrival of videotape technology, which facilitated the acquisition of more economical foreign productions, whose production costs had already been amortized in the original country (Vampre, 1979). The whole industry, however, had a regional character, with a commercialization structure and programming strategies that did not attend to the needs of advertisers, who wanted a national audience. As Browne says:

> Large nations might be expected to favor the development of regional and/or local services, particularly if there is an uneven distribution of the population. The Unite States, Canada, Australia and Brazil all seemed fairly indifferent to the development of national systems during the early years of broadcasting in their countries, although by late 1920s the United States had developed a clear channel system of frequency allocation that would bring at least a few stations to even the most geographically isolated listeners during nighttime (Browne, 1989, p.4).

The marketing environment in which the Brazilian networks were created started to be defined, though, only after 1964. Without the creation of a national telecommunication infrastructure and the deep economical changes promoted by the military regime instituted in that year, mass television would probably have remained restricted to very few cities. Browne comments:

> The more uneven the distribution, the harder for a large country to furnish a universal broadcast service, unless there is a commitment to some form of national service, as United States, Canada, Australia and, much later, Brazil, all eventually realized (Browne, 1989, p.6).

The drive to implement a national communication infrastructure would only be supported by a governmental policy more concerned about the integration of the country and ideologies than with commercial reasons. In terms of a consumer market, the advertisers would be expected to only target the audience that can participate in the consumption proposed by the mass media and advertising industries. Since expansion and investment is not necessarily compensated by a larger or more affluent audience, the coverage of areas away from the large urban centers would probably be economically negative to broadcasters. In ideological and institutional terms, on the other hand, a general mass audience would make more sense, and the military governments assumed the task of building the National Telecommunication System and a Mass Cultural Industry.

In 1968, Embratel (Empresa Brasileira de Telefonia)—a mixed capital company created three years before to control the long-distance telecommunications—premiered the National Microwave Network and the satellite transmissions that brought to Brazil the image of the man on the moon. On September 1, 1969, "Jornal Nacional," the first program transmitted in national simulcast chain, marked the beginning of network television in Brazil, followed in 1972 by the first color broadcasting. After 15 years of existence, the original TV stations in São Paulo and Rio de Janeiro became production centers, distributing their programming to other stations across the country. New regulatory agencies, like the Ministry of Communications created in 1967, reduced the interference of private organizations and reinforced the official influence on the Brazilian media in general. Decree 236, of February 28, 1967, changed CBT, excluding foreign control of telecommunication companies and limiting to ten (five VHF and five UHF) the number of stations one could own in the country (Melo, 1985). In many aspects, the Brazilian military adopted most of the American legislation. Likewise, a concession period of ten years for radio and 15 years for television could be renewed for equal successive periods, as long as the licensees "complied with all legal and contractual duties, maintaining the same technical, financial and moral characteristics."

Contrastingly, the President would give concessions after hearing the National Telecommunications Council and would also play the role of censor, defining the messages that could be transmitted. Until the 1988 Constitution, no major change was made in such laws, except for the restrictions that were imposed with Institutional Act 5, between 1968 and 1979. During the government of Emílio Garrastazu Médici (1969-1974), a National Security Law allowed the Executive the right to censor and stimulate auto-censorship to avoid prosecution. The existing concessions were threatened with cancelation and the new ones were restricted to groups that supported the government (Melo, 1985).

But the heavy State influence on Brazilian TV has actually extrapolated the legal and technical grounds. Its direct and indirect participation in the advertising revenues has also been significant. Even in 1982, LEDA (Levantamentos Econômicos de Dados de Anunciantes) data indicated that the federal government was responsible for more than half of the advertising investments in television, which totaled 5.7 percent of the Cr$ 34.7 billion invested in advertising in that year (LEDA, 1983). Mattos further indicates that the close relationship between banks and government made broadcasters' financing strategies subject to political control. And since they also depend on government licenses and subsidies to import equipment, says Mattos, most 36 companies have aligned their interests to that of the State (Mattos, 1990).

Indirectly, the promotion after 1964 of a quick industrialization process centered in large cities benefited television. In contrast to the American drive to the suburbs, which greatly enticed the development of alternative distribution systems like cable TV, the Brazilian mass audience was getting more and more concentrated in a few large metropolitan areas. This increased the penetration of electronic media, while at the same time artificially allowing the capital accumulation necessary to make the audience more upscale. With the establishment of direct credit to the consumers in 1968, this audience was allowed to consume more, including more TV sets, whose sales increased 48 percent in comparison to the previous year (Sodre, 1981).

Advertisers, advertising agencies and broadcasters were quick to turn the advantages into profits, putting Brazilian TV in fourth place (after USA, Japan and England) in percent participation of total advertising investment. The establishment of the national networks put broadcasters in a better position to negotiate. The time slots had their value raised and advertisers lost their control of the whole program. Since TV penetration was also higher, advertisers, on the other hand, enjoyed a reduced cost per thousand viewers. Large multinationals in the sectors of luxury products, commerce and banks were the most attracted to television. According to "Veja" magazine, in 1969 about 16 of the 24 soaps produced had the sponsorship of multinational companies like Gessy-Lever, Colgate-Palmolive and Kolynos-VanEss (1969a). The advertising agencies, as their token, had a 20 percent commission of broadcasting charges guaranteed in 1966 by decree number 57.690. According to Bolaño, the Brazilian market had grown in interest by the international agencies:

> The 70s were years of many changes in the advertising industry, including the lowest participation of the large multinational agencies ... since the 50s, their golden age in the country. In the 80s, this trend is reverted in favor of the national agencies, indicating that the barriers to entry previously established were very weak (Bolaño, 1988, p.41).

Taking full advantage of this favorable environment, TV Globo (another creation of the 1964 military movement) revolutionized the market, exerting in many ways a practical monopoly. With the financial and technical support of the American Time/Life Group, Globo transferred and adapted American know-how in the areas of administration, production and programming. It introduced new commercial practices—sponsorships, vignettes, breaks, etc.—that developed the market from a radio-like one (Furtado, 1988). Herbert Fiuza, member of the first Globo crew, declared: "Globo was inspired in an Indianapolis station, WFBM. And the engineer from that station was the one that installed it all, because we didn't know anything" (Filho, 1976). Between 1965 and 1970, the barriers to entry created by the stations of the first phase were gradually destroyed by Globo, which started to adopt a strategy of consolidation of its own barriers after 1970. According to Litman, "structural barriers may take many forms: economies of scale, absolute costs, product differentiation, barriers to exit and government rules, regulations and favors" (Litman, 1991, p.11); and Globo took advantage of all of them.

In the 1970s, the stability of the television market and the economic growth of the country allowed the survival of the smaller channels, aimed at audiences with lower acquisitive power, and whose programming included all the low-brow programs Globo discarded in the process of defining its quality standard. In the 1980s, the competition pattern changed again and it was possible to see the beginning of the end for the mass marketing environment and the total dominance of Globo (Bolaño, 1988).

2.1 The beginning of the end

Before the second half of the 1950s, says Nelson Hoineff, the network system had already been consolidated in the United States, being copied by other countries, while independent stations were disappearing (Hoineff, 1991). The "1970 Broadcast Yearbook" reported an 18.1 percent gross profit before taxes for the typical VHF station. And almost 40 percent of the total income went to the Big Three broadcasting networks (NBC, CBS and ABC). About 15 advertisers provided one third of this income, and the concentration of products of general, rather than specific interest, encouraged TV to have the broad, widest possible audience appeal (Schramm & Alexander, 1973).

Until 1976/77, however, there were only two TV networks in Brazil: Globo and the pioneer Tupi. The giants of previous years—Excelsior and Record—posed no threat anymore. The first was closed in 1970, and Record lost its network, being restricted to a regional group of three stations in São Paulo State (Bolaño, 1988). TV Bandeirantes had appeared in São Paulo in 1967, appealing to an elite audience, but a fire in its studios two years later forced it to use cheap foreign films to stay in business. In 1977, Bandeirantes opened another station in Rio de Janeiro—TV Guanabara—initiating a third network. On July 14, 1980, Tupi's stations were dispossessed by the government, in payment of the company's debts, and the concession was canceled. Two days later, president João Figueiredo closed seven of Tupi's stations and on July 23, opened the former Tupi licenses for applications for two new networks (a total of nine stations were distributed, including two other ones). SBT (Sistema Brasileiro de Televisão), which started in 1974 with TV Studios of Rio de Janeiro and had already acquired some of Record's stations, was one of the winners, initiating operations in the same year. The old, traditional Bloch Publishing Group initiated TV Manchete in 1983. Thus, the Brazilian market entered 1991 with 229 stations grouped in four national private networks—Globo (78), SBT (45), Manchete (38) and Bandeirantes (32)—two regional networks (Record/SP and Brasil Sul/RS), the State network Educativa (21), and 15 independent stations (Melo, 1992). In 1992, the popularesque OM network, the first to start outside the Rio-São Paulo circuit initiated operations with 10 stations. Based on low-brow programming such as theatre-like shows and Latin soap operas, the network of the Martinez family, who had been accused of receiving government funds in return for the support of Collor presidency campaign, reached the whole country with signals generated from Curitiba (Paraná state). In his book "Mercado Brasileiro de Televisão," Cesar Bolaño reviews the marketing history of the four large national networks, which are briefly summarized here:

Globo

The negotiations between Roberto Marinho, owner of "O Globo" newspaper in Rio de Janeiro and the American Time/Life Group (now Time/Warner), started in 1962, but the first station only came up in 1965 in Rio, followed by another in São Paulo in the next year. The importance of this contract was the flow of capital necessary to implement a competitive system around $5 million—and also the technical orientation. A Brazilian Congressional investigation determined that Time/Life not only technically assisted Globo, but actually managed and controlled all its assets, which was illegal. A nationalization process was demanded in 1969 and, two years later, Globo was declared to have paid all its debt to the American partner. According to Bolaño's interpretation, Globo succeeded because, besides Time/Life, there was national capital to be invested in this area and the political conditions were favorable. There was no interest by the government in treating Globo the same way as Excelsior. Globo's barriers to entry after 1970 were based on the adoption of a high standard of quality (the so called Globo Quality Standard), national network programming and a new commercialization system.

Due to the legal ownership limit of five stations in Brazil, Globo expanded with the inclusion of several affiliates. The affiliation contracts determined that Globo would furnish the programming for free, requiring only the maintenance of its quality standard. The national slots' revenues would be equally shared and the local ones were exclusive to the affiliates. In 1975, Globo's revenues were estimated at $230 million, or 0.35 percent of the Brazilian gross national product. About 85 percent of the revenues came from the commercialization of primetime slots, which enjoyed a captive audience around the evening soap operas. The high quality standard and the general appeal of the soaps allowed an impressive external expansion. The first Globo production to reach the international market was the soap "O Bern Amado" of 1976, which was sold to 17 countries in Latin America. In 1977 "Gabriela" was exported to Portugal and to the Portuguese-speaking African countries. Throughout the 1980s, the number of countries buying Brazilian productions doubled from 50 to more than 100 (Melo, 1988).

SBT

Until 1974, Silvio Santos was the host of a popular variety show aired by Globo, mixing "The Wheel of Fortune" and other American game shows with singer presentations and other typically Brazilian radio-type shows. In that year, he managed to open TV Studios station in Rio de Janeiro, while at the same time transferring "The Silvio Santos Show" to the competitor Tupi Network. In the following year, he acquired some of Record's stations and Santos' show started to be illegally aired in São Paulo simultaneously by Tupi and Record. Initially, his Sunday show was the only valuable programming of the incipient group of stations and there was not a strong effort to compete. Repetition of the same movie at different times of the day was done to create the tuning habit. In 1977, the production of the show was expanded to other genres, like soap operas, which also started to be sold to stations in other states. Working as a producer-syndicator-broadcaster, much as Fox was doing more recently in the United States (Head & Sterling, 1990), Silvio Santos Group even resold American movies purchased with nationwide exhibition rights (Bolaño, 1988).

In this manner, the new affiliated stations were not buying the packaged programming of a leader station, but individual programs. And instead of adopting Globo's strategy of exchanging programming for advertising slots, TVS worked as a distributor, receiving payments in cash. When the government finally licensed Silvio Santos to operate some of the Tupi stations and launch the Sistema Brasileiro de Televisão (SBT), he had already operated for six months an informal network based on a central and independent production unit and the commercial representation of the affiliates to the national advertisers located in Rio and São Paulo. The network quickly became the second in the ratings and, in August 1982, it surpassed Globo in São Paulo during the afternoons—something that had never occurred before. Since then, SBT has introduced romantic, traditional Mexican style soaps, importing many of them and producing others at low cost. Using low-brow, poorly produced programs aimed at the lower classes, SBT had a good performance in the early 1980s, even though the buying power of the lower classes had been drastically reduced. Indeed, the ratings success of SBT was not followed by an advertising success, since the audience had a lower buying power and the hideous character of the programs was incompatible with the advertisers' public image.

In Bolaño's interpretation, SBT's success can be attributed to their use of a leading product, "The Silvio Santos Show," and to a vertical integration of the Group's companies that cross-subsidized the network by advertising to prospective consumers, whose profile coincided with the network's audience. In 1983, SBT initiated some changes to convince the advertisers that its target audience also consumed. The argument was that the socio-economic segmentation did not consider the people with little education (an aspect overemphasized by ABA/ABIPEME), but high acquisitive power. New programming was added, like journalism and sports, and the old formulas of the shows suffered significant changes In 1985, the illegal situation in São Paulo was settled with the sale of Record's shares to the newspaper Jornal do Brasil of Rio de Janeiro.

Bandeirantes

As a participant in the elaboration of the Excelsior network, the founder of Bandeirantes, João Saad, always aspired to carry on its magnificent project. London BBC served as a model of infrastructure for Bandeirantes and the most modern concepts of television were studied in different parts of the world. But after the fire in 1969, the São Paulo station that had opened two years before became a simple exhibitor of imported movies and other cheap programs. There was no prospect of competing for audiences, but Bandeirantes enjoyed a positive public image in the 1970s as an alternative TV station programmed to masculine audiences of the upper classes at night. At that time, the movie programming was enhanced by music shows and a more analytic journalism than Globo's. Press companies like Jornal do Brasil, Abril, and Gazeta Mercantil produced programs for Bandeirantes under operational agreements. In 1977, the opening of TV Guanabara in Rio de Janeiro marked the beginning of the creation of a national network that would compete with Globo. However, instead of going after programs and audiences discarded by Globo, as SBT did, Bandeirantes tried to directly compete with the giant.

The impossible strategy was never fully implemented and the network lost its identity. In the beginning of the 1980s, Bandeirantes started losing audience to the low-brow programming of SBT and adopted a popularesque line of programming, contracting many important show hosts. The decline continued and in January 1981, Bandeirantes hired Walter Clark, considered by many as the guru behind Globo's success. Clark emphasized "regional productions, independent productions, upscale journalism for upscale audiences," but even though the ratings climbed among the elites as he intended, the Saad family dismissed him. Due to excess change in programming, unsuccessful experiences, and changes in the time of soaps, the total audience was significantly reduced during his administration. Thus, Bandeirantes had three distinctive perspectives in regard to its audience: a large national network, competing with Globo; a large national alternative network with popular programming, competing with SBT; and an alternative network with high-brow programming, later competing with Manchete. It was only after 1983, with the success of the sports programming provided by independent producer Luciano do Vale, that Bandeirantes started to recover, repositioning itself as the sports channel (Xavier Filho, 1991).

Manchete

On June 5, 1983, about two years after it was licensed—the maximum period for station implementation—TV Manchete of Rio de Janeiro premiered with promises to beat Globo's quality programs. Bloch Publishing Group, whose publications (including Manchete magazine) were in decline, invested $50 million to enter the market. About $27 million were consumed in sophisticated equipment that, for the first time, would put a network in a position to compete technologically with Globo (Meio & Mensagem magazine, February 1983). Even though the initial broadcasting was still limited to seven hours a day, in the first year Manchete took audiences away from Globo, SBT and, mainly, Bandeirantes, besides incorporating five percent of new TV sets in São Paulo and ten percent in Rio de Janeiro. The lower rating in São Paulo was explained by the regionalist character of the network and by tougher competition for upper class public, which was also targeted by the local stations Cultura and Gazeta. Surveys indicated that 52 percent of Manchete's audience was from classes A and B[3], and 23 percent had college degrees (Meio & Mensagem magazine, May 1984). Manchete's news bulletin was rated second in the country. To attract new viewers, it presented extensive news and recent Hollywood movies, but the success was ephemeral, since Globo counterattacked with even more expensive movies and small adaptations in its schedule.

---

3 The social classes in Brazil are traditionally divided in a scale from A to E.

Manchete only became a real threat to Globo between 1984 and 1985, when it started to produce mini-series and soaps. The evening soap "Pantanal" conquered in 1990 many viewers for Manchete's ten o'clock schedule, and forced Globo to recognize one of the first real threats in the soaps segment, which Globo mastered a long time ago. Without a long-term marketing structure, however, Manchete has not been able to profit from such successes. In 1990, it made $100 million just to spend almost the same amount, accumulating chronic debts and a tragic history of mismanagement. Every now and then, the press used to report a new attempt by 82-year-old Adolpho Bloch, owner of Manchete Group, to sell the network for the best offer. While the sale never happened, a debt of $50 million and scarce ratings successes doomed the network that once promised to debunk Globo's market leadership (1991p).

3

The Broadcast Nets Environment

To succeed in our overcommunicated society, a company must create a position in the prospect's mind. A position that takes into consideration not only a company's own strengths and weaknesses, but those of its competitors as well (Ries &Trout, 1981, p.29).

In the 1980s, the first signs of definitive market segmentation started to be visible in Brazil and America. The traditional television systems started facing strong competition and were forced to adapt to the new times, when industry entrants practice segmentation to establish their own market positions. In the United States, the broadcasting networks lost considerable percentages of their audiences to the growing cable networks, while the new Fox station lured away the younger audience niche. The so called Big Three (NBC, CBS and ABC) had enjoyed, until then, the benefits of an early entrance into the television industry, exercising minimum effort to keep their leading place in the market. In the words of Ries and Trout, "consumers are like chickens. They are much more comfortable with a pecking order that everybody knows about and accepts." The new cable networks, on the other hand, had the entering company's responsibility to detect alternative ways of doing business and of attracting audiences. In "Marketing of War," Ries and Trout applied military strategy terms to the entrant's task. They argue that the market leaders are at the top of a hill and that the entrants in the valley should not make a frontal attack on them, but use guerrilla tactics to conquer the flanks of the hill (or market). Translating: entrants should choose a market segment (or flank) not strongly controlled by the leaders and should carve their positioning step by step (Ries & Trout, 1987). That was exactly what the cable networks did by focusing their program schedules and audiences into specific niches that they detected as large and profitable enough to sustain their operations. Instead of going after a mass audience, which the advertisers associated in their minds to the Big

Three, the entrants sought new leading positions in the submarkets of music-lovers, news-followers, weather-watchers, etc. In each of the new sub-markets, each network was a leader and, even though their shares were not as big, the quality of their audiences attracted quality advertisers.

Continuing the war comparison, the entrants had conquered a flank the size of Monte Carlo and, while the enemy could still control the rest of the hill, they had one of the best pieces of the territory. The competition to the Big Three came not only from the new signal distribution technologies, but also from within the regular broadcasting industry. In 1980, for example, while the networks' audience share declined four percent, independent stations enjoyed an equivalent rise in primetime audience, bringing an increase in advertising revenues of 17 percent, compared to only 11 percent of the networks. The success of these stations could be attributed to strategic programming, like placing entertainment against news and vice versa, but it was also a reflex of laws limiting the network programming on affiliate stations, which turned them more independent. Each evening, the affiliates were forced to schedule their own programming (either internally produced or acquired from syndicators) in the half hour preceding the network primetime lineup (1977). Protecting the producers and the stations, laws like this actually turned out to be a problem for the networks.

Unlike the way it happens in Brazil, where the networks are the sole national production center of television programs (independent producers were only recently growing), the American networks could not count on the strength of their programming as a business bargaining tool. On the contrary, while the studios had greatly increased their prices, when the networks tried to pay less to studios and affiliates, the studios started to skip over the networks and negotiate directly with the stations (Grover & Liberman,1989). In this environment, it should be no surprise that a studio would enter the broadcasting business and control every step. In October 1985, Australian-American publisher Robert Murdoch announced the creation of Fox Broadcasting Company, which, counted together with the extensive film library of 20th Century-Fox Studios and six stations across the country, reached about 20 percent of all U.S. TV households.

Since the1960s, when United Network tried to enter the field and failed in less than one month, Fox represented the first competition for the other older networks, even though the initial results were rather disappointing. With the weakest stations in their markets as affiliates and an average audience of two to six percent, the network lost about $80 million in its first year (Head & Sterling, 1990). Nevertheless, Fox has been obtaining very positive results with a lineup targeted at younger audiences, which were revealed to be unattended to by the family programming offered by the Big Three. Interestingly, the younger audience is considered the most attractive one by advertisers, who have detected youth's higher willingness and acquisitive power to consume more. Thus, while the Big Three continued to suffer losses with their mass marketing, Murdoch's target marketing was proving successful. And, since Fox did not own enough stations nor cover most of the United States with all-day scheduling, it was not considered to be a network like the others; thus it escaped from many restrictive regulations that, for example, used to impede networks from syndicating their shows or having any profits from it.

Of course, the Big Three did not passively watch this loss of audience. Their main effort to counteract the loss had been to call for a revision of these restriction laws, called the Fin-Syn Rules. Over two decades before, the Financial Interest and Syndication Rules (§ 73.658-j) were included in Title 47 of the Code of Federal Regulations, prohibiting the networks—defined as offering 15 or more hours per week to at least 25 affiliated stations in ten or more states—from having financial interests or syndicating programs for non-network exhibition. The rules applied to the domestic market and, except for those programs produced solely by the networks, the international market also. The principle behind this prohibition was that the networks (the distribution industry) should not be allowed to integrate themselves vertically with the production industry and control the major stages of television activities.

A diversity of ideas would not be offered in this manner, and the public interest, convenience and necessity would not be attended to. On April 9, 1991, the Federal Communications Commission (FCC) approved a revision of the Fin-Syn Rules that, however, did not completely satisfy any of the parties. The networks continued to be precluded from selling shows in the domestic first-run area. On the other hand, they now could sell in-house and purchased-rights programs in the international syndication market, and could produce programs for first-run, which then had to be sold to a third-party syndicator for a producer's fee. But the FCC put a cap that did not exist before on the amount of in-house programming a network could schedule in primetime: 40 percent. In addition, the FCC won the right to seek a financial interest in, or domestic syndication rights to, primetime programs produced by outside producers (at least 20 percent participation). The networks claimed that their new rights had no value and that the studios were still too protected. They argued that few in-house primetime programs last long enough to be syndicated and that the producers would not sell foreign syndication rights. The producers were not happy either. The made-for-television movies and mini-series were not protected against the networks' extraction strategies, which could force the affiliates to clear the first-run syndicated programming they produced in-house. And the American producers would be facing foreign competition, as the new definition of in-house production allowed joint ventures with foreign entities.

The only happy faces seemed to be at Fox, which was now able to expand its primetime schedule to 15 hours a week (indeed, it quickly filled the primetime of every day of the week) without being considered to be a network (Duarte, 1991). There was still about ten percent of the market (TV households minus homes passed by cable) that did not have and may never have cable television, and the free programming offered by the broadcasting networks is watched by a considerable mass audience (1992a, p.1-A). Fox penetration had a significant slack to fill and the new FinSyn Rules were likely to keep the Big Three healthy for years to come, but not without further adaptations by affiliates. Tom Jones, general manager of the ABC affiliate in Lansing (MI), suggested that local stations should concentrate their offers on one type of programming, avoiding competition whenever there is a strong leader in a certain segment. His station went through different programming lines in its two years of existence, being forced to drop the local news bulletin and finally finding a profitable and unoccupied niche in daytime entertainment for middle-aged women. His rationalization: "In the news segment, an older station had already established a strong position, and our investments could not convince

40

the public to change channels. But in our present niche, even if we are number two, we can make as much as the number one" (Jones, 1992).

3.1 Segmentation the Latin American Way

The signal distribution technologies (and their revolutionary concepts) that brought segmentation to the American market started to fully arrive in Brazil only in the second half of the 1980s. Subscription Television was finally regulated in 1988, Globo's Direct-broadcast Satellite system took off in the following year, and cable experiments have assumed greater proportions. Even the origination of alternative programs through UHF stations, a phenomenon that took place during the 1950s in America, was initiated in Brazil by MTV-Abril in 1988. But the preconditions for Brazilian market segmentation had been developing for quite a while before that. Since competition is one of the most important elements in producing the market breakdown (it is the entrants' responsibility to look for alternative ways of doing business), the reduced monopolization of Brazilian television by Globo Network can be taken as the first sign of a segmentation era. One of the most common versions proposed by scholars like Caparelli and Mattos implies that the same government willingness to let Globo pursue its dominance of the market also allowed for the appearance of new competitors. The government would have become afraid of the power accumulated by Globo network and started to promote the competition that was overlooked until the last decade (Caparelli, 1980).

On October 16, 1977, the director of the Department of Telecommunications of the Communications Ministry, Colonel Idalecio Nogueira, summarized the new position: "The government is against monopoly in television, because it reduces the quality of programming and, therefore, would stimulate the concession of new channels to increase the number of national networks in the country." In "Tupi: a Greve da Fome" (1982), Humberto Mesquita states that the creation of two other channels—SBT and Manchete—was justified by the existence of a virtual monopoly by Globo Network, which

41

supposedly did not practice monopolistic strategies, but which still did not have any competitor (Mesquita, 1982). Not by mere coincidence, the promotion of competition by the Brazilian government gained impulse with the end of the military regime. While the generals would be more worried about keeping a unified message, restricting the proliferation of message makers, the civil governments seemed to be using television concessions as political bargaining tools. The rapid expansion of the number of stations that was begun during the government of Juscelino Kubitschek intensified in the 1980s (See Table 1). In four years of government, President Sarney gave away approximately 90 stations, compared to 136 distributed in two decades of military regime. The 1988 Constitution established rules to avoid the political tone of the concessions. Even though conceding and renewing licenses remained an Executive task, it now depended on the Congress's approval. Paragraph 5 of article 220 in chapter V of the Constitution further prohibited the creation of monopoly/ oligopoly in the media industry (1988a).

Table 1 - TV stations licensed per year in Brazil

Year	Stations	Year	Stations
1956 - 1964	14	1982	08
1964 - 1969	23	1983	04
1969 - 1974	20	1984	12
1974 - 1979	47	1985	22
1979	07	1986	14
1980	04	1987	12
1981	11	1988	42

Source: Communications Ministry. Reproduced from Mattos, S.Um Perfil da TV Brasileira. Salvador, ABAP, 1990.

Moreover, the new legislation base allowed for the arrival of new distribution systems, like cable and subscription television, and UHF stations in the capitals, with strong fragmentation impact. In the words of Barnouw:

Early network broadcasting (first radio, then television) had been praised for its unifying influence: it was said to have united the nation and even brought the family together'. The cable [and all other TV systems for that matter] era obviously had a fragmenting effect. With multiple channels serving multiple tastes (and, in many homes, sets in various rooms) *I* the mass audience had been replaced by a whole spectrum of audiences large and small (Barnouw, 1990, p.495).

The technology behind these systems appeared in the last two decades and played a complex role in the market dynamics. Barnouw recollects, for example, how television apparatus like videotape was developed to overstep the large studios' walls, creating the figure of the small independent producer, who allied creativity and low costs to provide many of the present successful TV programs. Thanks to Japanese technology, videotape even reached households, where the viewers time-shifted regular television programs and played pre-recorded leased tapes that had become a major competitor in the industry. In America, where video became popularized by the end of the 1970s, $10 billion were spent in 1990 on videotape leases, exactly double the amount spent at the box offices. For each $100 the movie industry made in Brazil, $80 came from the rent of videotapes and only $20 came from the theaters. In the first years of the 1980s, the situation was reversed, but in 1987 the two sources tied: $90 million. In 1991, the prospects were to get $490 million from tapes and $125 million from the box offices (Nery, 1991).

In 1982, when domestic videotape recorder (VCR) fever took the country, a set cost a third of the cost of the cheapest car on the market. In 1991, almost a dozen sets were necessary to equal that one-third-of-a-car-cost, and an estimated 8 million VCRs were in Brazil. This means that about 25 percent of the 30 million color TVs in the country were connected to a VCR. It was the same percentage registered, for example, in Italy. In this ranking, the leaders were Japan, with 79 percent, and USA with 67 percent (Nery, 1991). The rental stores survived the instability of the economy in Brazil. The anti-recessive measures adopted by the government in 1986 caused an enormous multiplication of these businesses: from 1,800 in 1985, they rose to 4,500 in 1987. And the following recession of the early 90s led many of the suddenly unemployed to open rental stores at home. Even though not all of these inexperienced entrepreneurs were still in the market after a couple of years, there were 8,000 of these stores in the country, receiving 500,000 new tapes every month (Nery, 1991).

As an alternative to the regular television programming, the video industry greatly contributed to the fragmentation of the mass audience as the first new television technology to take over the Brazilian market. Another version of the facts proposed by Caparelli (1982) and Mattos (1990) simply associates the appearance of competition in the TV industry to the development of national capitalism. The entrance of new capital would be a normal consequence of the regular growth of the industry within the general economy. In fact, however, the economy was worse in the 1980s and the appearance of new capital in a time when demand (advertising budget) was tending to fall negatively affected all companies. Some even proclaimed: "There is not enough space for all the networks in the country today. If nothing changes, the remaining funds are not enough to maintain the other three networks [SBT, Manchete, Bandeirantes]. There will be a change in the network system and the failure of some nets are possible" (Bolaño, 1988).

Thus, while the entrants have seemingly invested in spite of the economy, it is possible to see a causal relationship between the economy and market segmentation. In the previous decade, the low salaries, the reduced number of jobs and the more restrictive credit to consumers prevented a great portion of the mass audience from consuming most of the products advertised on television. The companies that advertised during the so-called "miracle era," in which Brazil's growing economy supported a mass consumption, expected the market to become more sophisticated and to consume more. Frustrated, many of them decided to use alternative media with campaigns aimed at their specific target, which had higher CPM (cost per thousand viewers reached), but overall costs very reduced. The distribution of advertising investments in the last few years of the 1980s was evidence of this tendency (See Table 2). Following an international tendency, the commercial sales sector, largest advertiser in the country, elected the newspaper as its main medium to carry its advertising (53 percent) in 1990. And from 1990 to1991, Brazilian newspapers increased their advertising share from 33 to 35 percent, while TV fell from 52 to 49 percent (1992b).

Table 2 - Advertising Investment Shares in Brazil

Year	TV	Newspaper	Magazine	Radio
1991	49	35	10	05
1989	55.44	26.56	12.84	2.74
1987	60.8	13.2	16.3	6.2
1985	59.0	15.0	17.0	6.0
1983	60.6	13.3	12.2	10.5
1981	59.3	17.4	11.6	8.6
1980	57.8	16.2	14.0	8.1
1978	56.2	20.2	12.4	8.0
1976	51.9	21.1	13.7	9.8
1974	51.1	18.5	16.0	9.4
1972	46.1	21.8	16.3	9.4
1970	39.6	21.0	21.9	13.2
1968	44.5	15.8	20.2	14.6
1966	39.5	15.7	23.3	17.5
1964	36.0	16.4	19.5	23.4
1962	24.7	18.1	27.1	23.6

Source: Leda - Nielsen Serviços de Midia, and McCann-Erickson Brasil

It is simple to understand why media segmentation—and now television segmentation—has gained prestige among advertisers. As chapter 6 further describes, the Brazilian market has always been full of contrasts. Even though the wealth is concentrated in a handful of places and the profiles of the consumers are restricted to a few categories, television made no differentiation among the 28 million TV households counted in 1991 (1991g). As the buying power of the majority of the population declined, the broad audience reached by television, which used to be its best selling point, was becoming a waste. The target audience of the programs was seen to become different from the target audience of the advertising spots, and advertisers were starting to question why they were paying extra for audiences they could not use. They apparently realized that it is harder to convince the few TV viewers with acquisitive power to consume more than it is to convince the many qualified viewers of a focused medium to buy enough. Since only potential buyers are targeted by a focused medium, there is virtually no waste, whereas broadcasting, in addressing an audience composed of many individuals who would not be interested in the sales message of a certain advertising piece is wasteful. According to Schiffman and Kanuk: "Marketers do not create needs, though in some instances they may make consumers more keenly aware of unfelt needs." Thus advertising only works for those who have a previous need for the product or service offered (Schiffman & Kanuk, 1991). Paying more to insert an ad in primetime, because it airs to a larger audience (thus the more indefinite one), may not be the best strategy for an advertiser that targets only a specific, well-known, reduced public.

3.2 Brazilian Network Segmentation

Appearing in the 1980s, amidst the fragmenting environment described before and facing the strong control of the market by Globo, the new Brazilian networks had not much choice but to adopt market segmentation strategies to conquer niches not fully attended to by the leader. Noticeably, this was a situation radically different from the American market, where NBC, CBS and ABC share mass audiences without resorting to segmentation strategies. Except for the incipient Fox, the major networks were created before the 1940s and compose an oligopoly with no continuous leadership. In this sense, the Brazilian experience may be a better reference for other countries presently promoting competition through the addition of new networks. The criterion for the division of the market has been the viewers' social class, which supposedly indicates a comprehensive set of consumption behavior patterns and programming tastes. In the late 1970s, Globo was the most upscale network, followed by Bandeirantes, which sometimes surpassed it. When Manchete entered the market in 1981, it replaced Bandeirantes, which precipitously abandoned the qualified market already conquered, opting for a popularesque (low brow) lineup. Without a clear positioning, Bandeirantes lost its identity and could not compete with SBT for the lower classes niche. It was only later that the Association Luqui-Bandeirantes brought to the network a strong foothold on the sports segment. Thus, it is possible to draw the following segmentation chart:

Table 3 - Patterns of Brazilian media use by social class

Social class	TV Networks	Radio	Print Media
Elite (5 - 10%)	Manchete, Globo	FM msic	Elite papers, News magazine
Middle (15 - 20%)	Globo	FM music, talk	Elite papers, News magazines
Working Class (10 - 15%)	Globo, SBT	FM music, AM music, talk	Popular newspaper
Poor (50 - 60%)	Globo, SBT	AM music, talk	
Marginal (10%)		AM music, talk	

Source: Duarte, L.G. & Straubhaar, J. & Stephens, J. "Audiences, Policy and Cable Technology". In ICA, Miami, 1992.

A table like this seems to be in the heads of many advertising professionals, those who are responsible for allocating the advertisers' investments. According to Ries and Trout: "This ranking of people, objects and brands [and why not networks] is not only a convenient method of organizing things, but also an absolute necessity to keep from being overwhelmed by the complexities of life" (Ries &Trout, 1981, p.36). Just as viewers know which channel to tune to for their favorite programs, advertisers keep in mind a ladder (hierarchy) with the best media for their messages. Using a Consumer Behavior concept, they have an "evoked set," a group of specific channels to I consider in watching/advertising (Schiffman & Kanuk, 1991). Other channels and networks, like Record or Gazeta of São Paulo, among others not included in the above chart, would compose the total set of choices, but Globo, SBT and Manchete attracted most of the audience shares at any moment. Remarkably, while Manchete reached only ten percent of the population at most, and SBT was watched by up to 75 percent, Globo managed to draw its audience from practically all the class segments (considering that the marginal ten percent do not participate

47

in the consumer market). To become the market leader, Ries and Trout say "you just get there firstest with the mostest," and that is exactly what Globo did. In the 1970s—thus, before the creation of Manchete and SBT—Globo consolidated its leadership in the market by raising the quality standards of its programming and its overall institutional image.

Advertising at Globo was having a spot next to Hans Donner's world famous computer graphics, the best journalism and the most expensive programming, reaching the "most upscale mass audience" across the country. The quality standard was aimed at keeping a large audience while forcing competitors to invest more to enter the market (raising the barriers to entry). Eventually, however, it lost some public, especially from the lower classes, to the cheap low-brow programming of competitors. SBT was the most successful in collecting the program genres Globo discarded, becoming the number two network in the country: Since advertisers tend to target higher classes (with higher acquisitive power to consume), the large audience of SBT did not translate into revenues, at first. The turning point for Silvio Santos' network was marked by the effective use of a Ries and Trout principle: *"A competitor that wants to increase its share of the business must either dislodge the brand above [in the mental ladder] (a task that is usually impossible) or somehow relate its brand to the other company's position"* (Ries & Trout, 1981, p.37). During the regular programming, SBT in-house spots announced its primetime programming as an alternative to Globo' s. If the leader had a drama feature, the contender offered a comedy, and so on, in a typical counterprogramming strategy.

According to Eastman's definition, SBT's tactics were indeed appropriate to combat the power of Globo. "Most other strategies are intended to hold viewers who are already watching (flow strategies)," but the majority of the audience was tuned to Globo's soaps during primetime. Counterprogramming "interrupts flow to gain different viewers, making it an effective scheduling option, especially for the network facing a super hit program on another network" (Eastman, Head, & Klein, 1989. p.152). Better movies were purchased to attract new viewers and the weekly schedule was intensely announced in the commercial intervals. Globo counterattacked by extending the time of its evening soap operas—the second-best rated program in the country—but SBT put cartoons on the air until the soaps were finished. Santos was successful, because he acknowledged the general taste for the competitor's soaps and related its network to the leader by creating the habit of turning the channel afterwards for alternative programming. In terms of positioning, SBT was assuming the second place in the ranking and consolidating it, much as Ries and Trout prescribe: "For 13 years in a row, Avis [car leasing] lost money. Then they admitted that they were No. 2 and Avis started to make money ... [Their slogan was] Avis is only No.2 in rent-a-cars, so why go with us? We try harder" (Ries & Trout, 1981, p.38). The *"No. 2"* positioning conquered the market (for advertisers, besides viewers) in the provocative campaigns designed by advertising wizard Washington Olivetto (See Figure 1).

Figure 1 – SBT's Vice Leadership Ad

Source: VejaSP, May 6, 1992.

Text: We are the Vice. And We Assume. Audience Share – São Paulo 6:00/24:00. Monday through Friday. First Semester 1992. ADP-IBOPE Report. Absolute and Assumed Leader of the Vice-Leadership.

Famous worldwide in advertising, Olivetto had previously created similar campaigns, emotionally involving the target and taking advantage of the Brazilian tendency to sympathize with the less fortunate. Just as he had made history with TV spots for *Bom Bril* cleaning pads or São Paulo gas stations, SBT campaigns in the printed media forced Globo to advertise itself (in other media) for the first time—and with a rather defensive tone. Some Brazilian TV critics (Silva, 1982) said that Globo decreased its standards of quality programming as a defensive strategy against SBT. According to Bolaño, however, the leader's strategy regarding the target audience never changed. It introduced programming and show hosts of more popular taste, but the standards remained high. He explains that the strategy was more like a show of force, balancing the programming to indicate to the audience that the competitors cannot offer anything Globo does not (Bolaño, 1988).

A reverse example Bolaño mentions was when Manchete premiered with a long list of top-rated movies and Globo counterattacked with even more premium movies. With promises to go after the leader, Manchete never achieved enough success to pay the huge debts of its creation. While rumors of a buyout were constant, the network soon found out that investments in technology were worthless without quality personnel. Significant salaries attracted some key professionals from Globo and Manchete finally scored in 1990, with the soap opera "Pantanal," whose slow pace, nudity and beautiful scenery of Central-west Brazil reached a 40 percent audience share. Since it was aired at a different period (later at night), "Pantanal" managed to have more audience than Globo's programming without confronting the competitor's main programs: the eight o' clock national news bulletin ("Jornal Nacional") and the subsequent soap opera. Thus, in the segment of "telenovelas" (soap operas), Manchete found a niche in the ten o'clock period that was not dominated by the leader and successfully controlled it. Counter-programming "Pantanal," Globo changed the schedules of programs, introduced big box-office movies at the ten o'clock period and put more nudity in its telenovelas, but in1991 the segment would suffer another attack, this time from SBT. Imported from Mexican Televisa for $10,000 a chapter, "Carrossel" reached 21 points against 41 of "Jornal Nacional" at the eight o'clock period. This time, there was not much Globo could do.

In the past, there was a war of "telenovelas," now the competing products were different. It is a fact everywhere that entertainment programs always beat news bulletins, exception made to situations like wars, etc. Afraid of a programming war that would annihilate their news programs, the three American networks have long ago sealed a gentleman agreement, airing their nightly news bulletins at the same time. In 1988, during his show, Silvio Santos made a proposal to the other channels to follow the American example, but he did not succeed. Because of the lack of competitors with the same level of equipment and resources, Globo had no reason to accept the offer. Its three news programs were among the five largest audiences of the network (1991c). In 1985, the SBT launched the Mexican children's comedy "Chaves" to compete with the regional news bulletins of Globo. This strategy worked relatively well and in the early 90s the program averaged nine percent of the audience. Thus, using a variety of marketing strategies, the other networks seemed to be drawing a pattern of more frequent programming successes outside Globo, what was once impossible or very seldom achieved. In the 1970s, Globo had "telenovelas" with average audience around 70 percent, in the 1980s it was 60 percent, and it started 1991 with 50 percent.

The average throughout the 90s was around 41 percent (1991c). "Jornal Nacional" had an incredible average of 70 percent in 1983, fell to 64 percent in the following year and in 1991 was surprised by "Carrossel" with 40 percent. In the first five months of 1991, Globo went into debt by $20 million and, while the apparent decline of Globo's dominance led some to envision better and more diversified Brazilian television programming, others became worried (1991c). As Browne reminds, "in competing, stations may lower the quality of their services in order to cut costs and may drop programs that attract small audiences, no matter how devoted those audiences may be" (Browne, 1989, p.17). Indeed, some of the most recent Globo programs had assumed a more low-brow character, even though it still invested much more than the other networks (which implied the need for higher returns). The preoccupation was that competition with the cheap imported programs of its rivals could drive Globo out of its more sophisticated productions. Each chapter of a telenovela costs an average of $30,000—three times more than any Mexican soap. The only thing that Globo exhibited that it did not produce itself was movies; more than 80 percent of its programming came from its studios, a very rare case in the world (1991c). But Globo had long prepared itself for a scenario of increasing competition, not only from other networks, but also from other TV distribution systems. In marketing terms, the market leader brilliantly performed Ries and Trout's recommendations:

> The leader should cover all bets ... [they should] swallow his or her pride and adopt every [competitor's] new product development as soon as it shows promise ...time is of essence if a covering move is to be effective. You want to block the competitor by moving aggressively to cover the new product before it becomes established in the prospect's mind (Ries & Trout, 1981,p.57).

Globo anticipated the competition process and initiated some segmentation itself without losing its mass (or "global") character. Globo initiated a market study to identify the potential advertisers, which sectors they were in, what kind of public they were looking for, with what kind of messages, with what kind of service. Thanks to this move, Globo maintained and even increased its audience in the first half of the 1980s. In 1980 it started experimenting with the potential of some audience niches like children, housewives, men class *A/B* between 30 and 50, etc. The strategy to seek segments of the public at alternative schedules (out of primetime) had a frustrating beginning with the program "TV Mulher," which premiered on April 7, 1980 and was terminated shortly after. But other niches have been successfully conquered and the program formulas copied by the competitors: the country format ("Globo Rural" and "Som Brasil"), computer format ("Globo Informática"), educational format ("Zero a Seis" and "Globo Profissões"). In 1986, Globo further defined the strategies it would follow to cope with a scenario where its quasi-monopoly situation vanquish (1991c). Besides adopting *"a* positioning to use its immense resources to conserve the audience leadership whenever possible," (1991c) it studied various initiatives to diversify the businesses of the group.

Competing technologies, like videocassettes or subscription television, which promised to reduce the network audience and harm its business, were then integrated into the group's operation and, if necessary, Globo could cross-subsidize network productions. Illustratively, as the video market grew in Brazil, the new Globo Video started to market some movie titles and documentaries. Paulista and Rio Metro in the subscription television branch, and GloboSat in the direct broadcast satellite system, also marked the leader's foothold on the new industries. Similar diversification initiatives were taken by the other networks as well, following the international pattern to form communication conglomerates, present in every line of media. Since most of the Brazilian media companies are controlled by family groups, instead of many little shareholders as it happens in the United States, the conglomerate expansion took a very interesting line. The origins of Globo and other national conglomerates are usually associated with the printed media, while the new family generations were taking over the electronic media. The perfect example is Abril Group, whose founder, Victor Civita, got started printing Disney's Mickey Mouse comic books and his grandsons were later entering the subscription television business. In America, this expansion took a very different route. While the networks had their growth limited by law (to protect the public interest, convenience and necessity), the competing media systems were not restricted and grew faster to buy them out. Barnouw recollects how the competing media became simply branches of larger parent companies, many of them without even any communication background:

> The 1980s saw not only a battle of technologies but parallel battles at the corporate level ... Media were the choice targets; contenders included not only media organizations but conglomerates of all sorts seeking wider diversification, and convinced that communications had become the key to power and profit. [As networks were allowed to own 12 stations, they became targets of take-overs] achieved with borrowed capital. To cope with resulting debts, the takeovers were often followed by staff reductions (Barnouw, 1990, p.509).

Looking back in perspective, it is possible to say that the limitation of the American networks may have made feasible the appearance and progress of the competing television technologies, which could otherwise have been suffocated by more powerful networks in their efforts to maintain their business. Just as the studios tried to prohibit the sale of VCRs, the networks barred the quick expansion of cable, and cable operators were then lobbying against telephone companies delivering television. Different scenarios could have emerged. In Brazil, however, these technologies were arriving with a long delay and, since the companies already know their impact in the market and their possible profitability, the adoption of the new systems was expected to be much smoother. The Brazilian companies were not limited by the same American regulations and the expansion could happen within communication conglomerates, rather than across different lines of business.

4

Distribution Tech Segmentation

Another reason our messages keep getting lost is the number of media we have invented to serve our communication needs (Ries & Trout, 1981, p.16).

One of the major driving forces behind television segmentation is the multiplication of channels spawned by the evolution of new signal distribution systems. Once, the number of competing stations in a given market was limited by the over-the-air radio frequency spectrum available. And, considering only the original very high frequency (VHF) used, practical competition was actually reduced to a couple of stations, which targeted the complete universe of audience with rather similar programming. In 1952, the use of ultra high frequencies (UHF) and microwaves to broadcast or just relay the signals of distant stations introduced new competitors to the established markets. But to lure a captive audience as well as advertisers away from the existing stations, the entrants would have to offer something different. Even if a similar lineup was adopted, a new batch of sitcoms, news bulletins, talk shows, etc., reached the airwaves. The fate of most segmented television enterprises in the market is more connected to the success of their programming than to the attractiveness of the technology adopted to deliver it. The increase of choices continued with the development of distribution systems like STV (Subscription Television), MDS (Multipoint Distribution Service), MMDS (Multichannel Multipoint Distribution Service), DBS (Direct Broadcast Satellite) and cable. At that point, however, there was not enough mass audience—nor advertisers—for every entrant and the programming had to attend to only a part of the market.

In Brazil, the introduction of some new signal distribution technologies only occurred in the last decade of the century, and the amplification of choices was still an ongoing process (See Figure 1). In this chapter, the development of some distribution systems is reviewed as benchmarks for the Brazilian operations, which have often imported

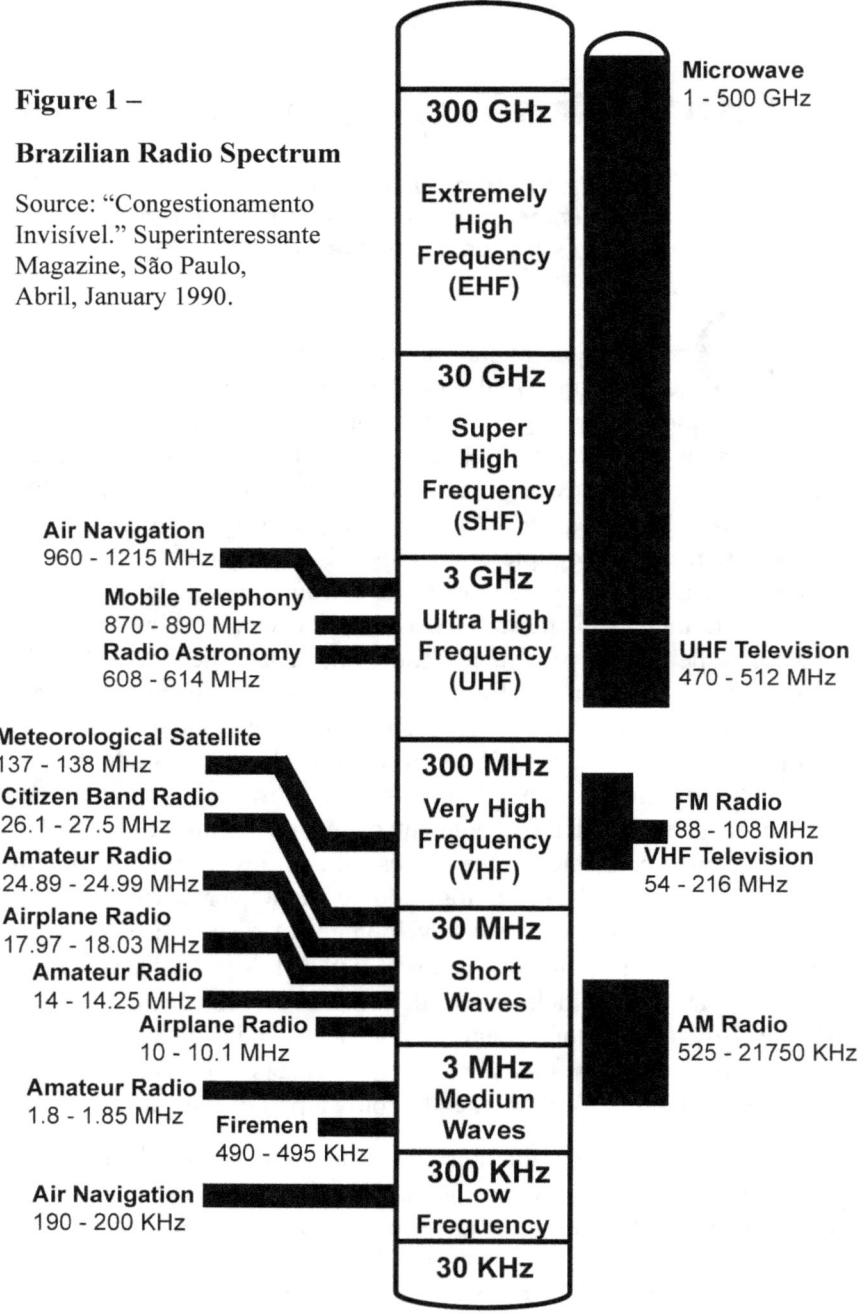

Figure 1 –

Brazilian Radio Spectrum

Source: "Congestionamento Invisível." Superinteressante Magazine, São Paulo, Abril, January 1990.

Microwave
1 - 500 GHz

300 GHz

Extremely High Frequency (EHF)

30 GHz

Super High Frequency (SHF)

Air Navigation
960 - 1215 MHz

Mobile Telephony
870 - 890 MHz

Radio Astronomy
608 - 614 MHz

3 GHz

Ultra High Frequency (UHF)

UHF Television
470 - 512 MHz

Meteorological Satellite
137 - 138 MHz

Citizen Band Radio
26.1 - 27.5 MHz

Amateur Radio
24.89 - 24.99 MHz

Airplane Radio
17.97 - 18.03 MHz

Amateur Radio
14 - 14.25 MHz

Airplane Radio
10 - 10.1 MHz

Amateur Radio
1.8 - 1.85 MHz

Firemen
490 - 495 KHz

Air Navigation
190 - 200 KHz

300 MHz

Very High Frequency (VHF)

FM Radio
88 - 108 MHz
VHF Television
54 - 216 MHz

30 MHz

Short Waves

AM Radio
525 - 21750 KHz

3 MHz

Medium Waves

300 KHz
Low Frequency

30 KHz

technologies and concepts without an overall national blueprint. The segmentation of the programming by the entrants in the Brazilian market is discussed in chapter five. The future of each distribution system in Brazil was still impossible to forecast in the early 90s. The government seemed to have leaned toward STV and MMDS, although cable and DBS experiences were defying the odds and increasing market penetration. The competition had already started, but it seemed unlikely that some systems could preempt the chances of others, as it happened in America. As previously mentioned, programming proved to be of primary importance for attracting audiences. Importing American cable programming or producing its own, the companies made use of satellite relays and can easily switch the local distribution system as necessary. In any case, the higher implementation costs were likely to delay some systems more than others (See Table 1) and, in the environment of the early 90s, only a handful of enterprises could be taken as examples.

Table 1 – Systems' Implementation Costs in America

Cable	
Installation on existing utility poles - rural area	$10,000 per mile
Installation on existing utility poles - urban area	$100,000 per mile
Underground cable	$300,000 per mile
Channel capacity upgrade	$10,000 to 15,000 per mile
Color studio	$200,000 or more
PPV hardware	$10,000
Radio	
Small market AM/FM station	$50,000
Median equipment annual budget	$20,000
Broadcasting TV	
Full power, major market station	$30,000,000
Median equipment annual budget	$300,000
Satellite	
Construction and launch	$200,000,000
Transponders lease, per month	$25,000 to 200,000

Transponders lease, per hour	$200
Earth station (uplink) construction	$600,000 to $750,000
Uplink hourly lease (C Band)	$396
Uplink hourly lease (Ku Band)	$480
TVRO dishes	$1,000 to 40,000
SMATV	
300 UNIT SYSTEM (including $35,000 for Earth	
stations, but excluding cabling)	$80,000
MMDS	
Per subscriber	$600

Source: Head, Sydney W. and Sterling, Christopher H. "Broadcasting in America: A Survey of Electronic Media." Boston, Houghton Mifflin Co. Sixth Edition, 1990.

4.1 The ultra high expectations toward UHF

The use of ultra high frequencies was not exactly new in Brazil. In 1957, television broadcasting reached the countryside of São Paulo state through UHF retransmission stations. In the United States, similar intercity relay systems have been in operation since 1950, using microwave frequencies around 6 or 7 GHz in the super high frequency(SHF) portion of the spectrum (Tessman, 1992). According to Brazilian engineer José Roberto Cappia, a telecommunications consultant in São Paulo, the process was simple and had still been in use. The main station in the capital broadcast locally through a very high frequency (VHF) transmitter antenna within the metro area. At the same time, another antenna in the outskirts of the city captured these signals and converted them to UHF, which were rebroadcast to stations in other cities. Thanks to the variation of frequencies and the concentration of UHF signals in a point-to-point basis, the interference is eliminated and every station can relay the signals to even more distant localities (See figure 2).

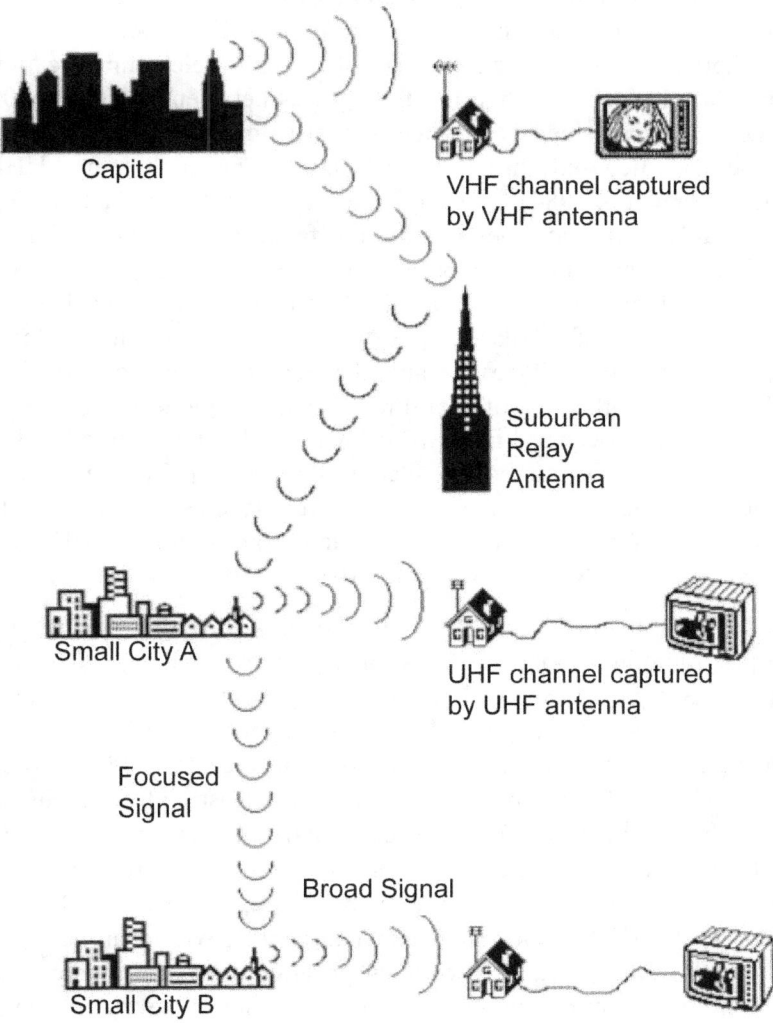

Capital

VHF channel captured
by VHF antenna

Suburban
Relay
Antenna

Small City A

UHF channel captured
by UHF antenna

Focused
Signal

Broad Signal

Small City B

Figure 2 – UHF Relay System

The major problem with such a sequential network, as Cappia indicates, is the possibility of breaking one of the links and cutting communications with all the cities connected from that point on. More recently, the implementation of a satellite-based network provided

59

for a wider and more reliable coverage of the Brazilian territory, as described in the following sections (Cappia, 1992). Decree 4.1117 of August 27, 1962 instituted the Brazilian Telecommunication Code; article four classified the frequencies between 300 and 3,000 MHz as UHF services. Nevertheless, the list of commercial stations in operation licensed until 1967 in Brazil did not include any UHF station (Sampaio, 1984). The origination of signals by a UHF station presumably started at cities that are too far from a capital station to receive its signals, but too close to interfere with its signals, in case another VHF broadcasting would take the airwaves. In technical terms, no two stations of similar frequency—co-channels—can be closer than 160-190 miles (1955c), because the area of interference (80 miles radius) is twice the area of useful reception. The pioneer experiment in such a mode occurred in New York City with VHF station WNBT and a UHF retransmitter, also called a "slave station," in Bridgeport, located 55 miles away. Using a microwave relayed signal, KC2XAK covered only 6 miles, and about a hundred homes received UHF TV sets provided by RCA to participate (Mann, 1950).

In 1982, there were 3,097 UHF stations in Brazil retransmitting the programming of one of the national networks in cities other than capitals (Sampaio, 1984). In the major metropolitan areas of the capitals, on the other hand, the earlier assignment of up to seven VHF channels left the need for UHF stations only to smaller centers, which could not interfere with the capital's predefined broadcasting frequencies. It was only in the mid-1980s that large capitals, like São Paulo and Rio de Janeiro, received concessions for UHF stations in order to allow for more than the existing channels. Abril Group then became the first licensee of a UHF station in a Brazilian capital, with channel 32 of São Paulo. The insertion of original programming in a market like São Paulo, where the public could already count on seven channels, implied a further fragmentation of the audience's attention. The new availability of channels made the audience options numerous enough that the expectation of a mass audience could not be realized by all competitors. And the expectation of smaller audiences in a segmented market justified the targeting of certain niches. This tendency toward special interest programming was realized by many American UHF stations in the 1960s. Most of them were not network affiliated and had to produce their own shows or buy cheap syndicated ones, usually opting for educational, ethnic or alternative schedules.

Some municipally owned stations, like WNYC (NY), KCET (CA) or WETA (DC), enjoyed relative success with mainly educational lineups. The ethnically-oriented stations were also very popular in some regions, with bullfights and soaps imported from Mexico. But, the commercial ones had more problems and, like Brazilian station Jovem Pan had been doing, they relied heavily on old movies and a lot of local sports (1966). A few stations aired non-conventional programming to become an alternative channel (1969b). New York's WUHF, for instance, used to broadcast the morning lineup of police prisoners four times a week—scrambled to 18 precincts (Tepfer, 1962). In any case, most of these American stations achieved relative success in a time when the military regime in Brazil had traced rather different goals than the American Federal Communication Commission (FCC). Some of the concerns in America were the multiplication of stations, enhancing competition and favoring a wider variety of programming options, especially including the local affairs. Meanwhile, the Brazilian military governments favored a few sympathetic enterprises, building a national infrastructure for their expansion. More than multiple voices, they were interested in unifying the country under a few certified communication channels. Thus, equivalent UHF experiences had to wait two decades for new democratic policies.

4.1.1 The democratization of the spectrum

The end of the military period in Brazil was followed by a great distribution of new television concessions, which allowed for the segmentation process of the 90s. The arguments of the past years that there was neither market demand nor capacity to sustain more channels had been easily debunked by Brazilian economics. The elite had long resented the low-brow character of mass television (Sodré, 1981), and the contemporary development of new stations was happening in the middle of one of the worst economic crises of the country.

Behind this modern proliferation of stations, it seems, was the increased use by the civil governments of television concessions as a political tool. In exchange for favorable votes to their political projects, the governments awarded many politicians with such concessions. One of the most transparent cases was the distribution of 418 licenses (1991r) by ex-president José Sarney to the members of Congress who supported the bill that maintained him in the government for five years[4]. The Departamento Intersindical de Assessoria Parlamentar (DIAP or Department of Inter-Union Parliamentary Assistance) calculated that, in 1991, among the 584 senators and deputies in the National Congress, more than 130 were owners of radio and television licenses. And this number is only a small fraction of the real one, which includes those politicians who registered the concessions under the name of friends or relatives (1991r). After the issue of the new Constitution Letter in October 1988, the process of conceding licenses to operate radio and television stations became more public. The law still attributed the concession decision to the Executive power, but Congress then had to validate such decisions. Afraid of Congressional "harassment," the Communication Ministry quickly gave away about 450 concessions in the nine months prior to the issue of the new letter—that is, one concession a day.

The initiatives used to avoid Congress seemed rather unnecessary a few years later. In 1991 the Senate approved, without any discussion, the distribution of 64 stations of radio and television, determined during the last days of the Sarney government. The 51 members of the Science, Technology, Informatics and Communication Commission of the Congress were responsible for evaluating the Executive's decisions, but their conflicts of interest were clear: at least 17 of them were also licensees (Sá, 1990). In total, Sarney distributed 1,316 radio and television stations during his government; 288 were sent to Congress for approval and only 185 were finally conceded.

Although engineers insist that both VHF and UHF frequency ranges have been used to the fullest in most of the important Brazilian cities

4 From 1964 to 1985, the military regime imposed indirect elections of the president of the republic. In 1985, the last indirect voting by-the Congress elected a civil government, composed by the governor of Minas Gerais, Tancredo Neves, and the situation party dissident José Sarney. The sudden illness and death of Tancredo Neves in that same year, just before the presidential ceremony, led Sarney to the presidency. As a vice-president, his government was legally restricted to four years.

(which would mean a maximum of seven VHF and ten UHF stations), the proportion of UHF stations was still restricted in comparison to the VHF. The most updated channel attribution plans found for this study in decree number 86 of September 26, 1990 (1990e) and decree number 90 of September 28, 1990 (1990f) confirm that the UHF could have more room to grow (See Table 2 and 3).

In the analyses of many media professionals, the practical problem was not the ownership of media by the politicians, but the use of the media for political purposes. In fact, the ownership of a media company or access to one is something most politicians consider as vital for the success of their political campaigns. In the absence of a Fairness Doctrine, as applied by the United States to assure an equal time to all candidates in the media, a Brazilian candidate can win or lose popularity depending on his/her ability to conquer media space. President Fernando Collor also used media concessions as political tool. In the beginning of his mandate, in 1990, he refused a proposal to adopt a random assignment every time there is more than one candidate for the same license. His Economy Minister and cousin, Zélia Cardoso de Mello, also benefitted from the politics of concessions: she was a partner in the first subscription channel of São Paulo, Canal+ (Sá, 1990). This political instrument became more abundant after July of 1991, when the government increased the number of licenses available in the country from 500 to 1,539 (1,376 for radio licenses and 163 for television). The compression in the radio and television frequencies (a real expansion in the number of stations) was justified so as to allow the government to meet the 1,000 applications that had accumulated in the Infrastructure Ministry, although it was really designed to open the door to more important markets.

The 103 licenses that Sarney did not distribute were located in some distant, politically less important parts of the country, but the reform promoted by Collor allowed the creation of new stations in rich and populous areas, from which many politicians draw votes (Cruz, 1991). Since the VHF spectrum is mostly taken in such areas, and new entrants are more likely to pursue specific segments of the market, the development of the UHF system and television segmentation became very intertwined in Brazil. The UHF system, however, has a history of developmental difficulties. Some of the problems are inherent in

63

the characteristics of the ultrahigh frequencies, but others are a mere reflection of the low value given to this service across the years.

Table 2 - Channel Distribution for Retransmission in Brazil

State	Total	VHF		UHF	
Acre	38	26	68%	12	32%
Alagoas	13	12	92	1	8
Amapá	11	10	91	1	9
Amazonas	91	91	100	0	0
Bahia	529	419	79	110	21
Ceará	240	218	91	22	9
Distrito Federal	3	0	0	3	0
Espírito Santo	27	14	52	13	48
Goiás	293	107	37	186	63
Maranhão	33	29	88	4	12
Mato Grosso	103	102	99	1	1
Mato Grosso do Sul	146	135	92	11	8
Minas Gerais	577	150	26	427	74
Pará	232	133	57	99	43
Paraíba	25	14	56	11	44
Paraná	457	79	17	378	83
Pernambuco	78	54	69	24	31
Piauí	185	111	60	74	40
Rio de Janeiro	68	15	22	53	78
Rio Grande do Norte	18	13	72	5	28
Rio Grande do Sul	551	211	38	340	62
Rondônia	43	43	100	0	0
Roraima	31	31	100	0	0
Santa Catarina	166	147	89	19	11
São Paulo	1391	113	8	1278	92
Sergipe	11	11	100	0	0
Tocantins	122	107	88	15	12

Source: Decree Number 90. September 28, 1990.

Table 3 – Basic plan of VHF/UHF channel distribution in Brazil

State	Total	VHF		UHF	
Acre	8	4	50%	4	50%
Alagoas	8	4	50	4	50
Amapá	8	4	50	4	50
Amazonas	10	6	60	4	40
Bahia	23	18	78	5	22
Ceará	10	6	60	4	40
Distrito Federal	10	6	60	4	40
Espírito Santo	17	13	76	4	24
Goiás	17	12	71	5	29
Maranhão	15	11	73	4	27
Mato Grosso	13	9	69	4	31
Mato Grosso do Sul	15	11	73	4	27
Minas Gerais	37	35	95	2	5
Pará	28	20	71	8	29
Paraná	36	30	83	6	17
Pernambuco	15	11	73	4	27
Piauí	9	5	56	4	44
Rio de Janeiro	26	23	88	3	12
Rio Grande do Norte	9	5	56	4	44
Rio Grande do Sul	40	38	95	2	5
Rondônia	12	8	67	4	33
Roraima	7	3	43	4	57
Santa Catarina	27	23	85	4	15
São Paulo	63	46	73	17	27
Sergipe	8	4	50	4	50
Tocantins	9	8	89	1	11

Source: Decree Number 86. September 26, 1990.

4.1.2 The UHF handicap

On July 1, 1952, the American Federal Communications Commission opened the ultra high frequency band of the electromagnetic spectrum to television broadcasting in the United States (See Table 3 above). After a five-year embargo on any permits, the Sixth Report and Order tentatively allocated 2,000 stations in 1,357 communities using 70 new channels (14 to 83). Together with the VHF stations, the television spectrum had been increased six times. Nearly all stations were for cities with populations of less than 50,000, and the goal was to increase competition to a national level, encouraging a wide choice of television programming in an era before cable. Indeed, the previous FCC policy of localism in the VHF television channel assignment had limited to three the number of possible networks in the country, and of 272 major markets, only 71 were served by three or more TV stations (1962b). With the addition of VHF stations as well, the combination should provide 2,000 TV stations within a few years (See Table 4) (1951), elevating to five or six the number of possible national networks (1962b).

Table 4 - 1952 Channel assignment in America

	VHF	UHF
Commercial	617	1,436
Educational	80	162

Source: Foster, E. "Understanding Broadcasting." Addison Wesley Pub., 1982

The FCC's enthusiasm for the UHF band was shared by the entrepreneurs. Two hundred of the 500 applications filed were for the less disputed new television band (1952). The first commercial UHF station to go on the air was KPTV in Portland, Oregon, on September 20, 1952. By November 1, 1953 there were 94 UHF stations in operation and the FCC had issued construction permits to 180 more (Hertzberg, 1954). However, such high expectations would soon fade as many stations folded. Two years after the UHF was opened, a comparison of the 135 UHF stations and the 151 VHF stations that got started in that period revealed very negative numbers. About 15 percent of UHF and 37 percent of VHF stations were making a profit; from the 77 permits never used. 64 were UHF and only 13 were VHF; and of the 12 who quit after getting on the air 10 were UHF and only 2 were VHF (1954a). In his book, "Understanding Broadcasting," Eugene Foster recollects this frustrated beginning:

> By the end of 1952 there were three UHF stations on the air and many were encouraged that within six months of the lifting of the Freeze, three applicants could get through all the red tape at the FCC, order and accept delivery on their equipment, and begin broadcasting. A year later the number had risen to 115 and there was reason for optimism. However, in the summer of 1953 there had been stories in the trade press about UHF stations that were encountering serious audience and financial problems. By the end of the year some had given up. The year-end figures for UHF stations on the air in the 1950s were:

Year	Number of Stations
1952	3
1953	115
1954	116
1955	102
1956	91
1957	84
1058	77
1959	76" (p. 133)

Indeed, the arrival of UHF stations, more than a decade after the FCC authorized television as a broadcast service, found a very inhospitable market. A *Newsweek* magazine article describes this late adoption of UHF:

> Experimentation in television began before World War II in the VHF range, because transmitters could not handle higher frequencies. The small VHF band was hemmed in by military frequencies, after

the war several engineers (including some at CBS) urged that TV be moved to the wider UHF band. But broadcasters and manufacturers, anxious to increase set production and programming, claimed that UHF equipment would be years in developing, and that TV should start commercial broadcasting in the VHF range. Somewhat reluctantly, the FCC agreed (1966).

By 1952 there were already 108 VHF stations in 63 of the United States' largest markets, broadcasting to more than 17 million households with antennas and receivers purchased for VHF only. Moreover, the Big Three networks had established a VHF infrastructure and, along with the TV set manufacturers, were said to be boycotting the UHF with fear that this frequency would take over the VHF (1962b). The FCC took a series of actions to alleviate such problems before realizing that the network option for VHF was actually conditioned by the advertisers' interest in the larger audiences delivered. In 1954, the Federal Commission added two UHF stations to the maximum of five each network could own (1954a), but after frustrated attempts, the networks quickly reaffiliated with their former VHF stations. The competition for VHF stations was especially difficult as the 1952 license "defrost" also allowed VHF stations to increase their power and coverage, reaching former UHF-only markets. The FCC's intermixture plan was designed to assure at least two stations in small markets and about seven in the larger ones, but the simultaneous growth of VHF seemed to limit the chances of UHF stations. The so-called "drop-in" authorized by the FCC allowed a VHF station to broadcast a directional signal from a neighboring town, without interfering with cities in other directions (1955c).

Later, the FCC also allowed VHF to extend coverage by operating up to five satellite and booster stations (1954b). Facing direct competition in 70 of the 100 top markets, many UHF stations encountered severe difficulties. General Electric, which had about $3 million tied up in UHF TV equipment that was yet to be paid for, launched a new company called National Affiliated Television Stations, Inc. The company was to give management advice, and provide sales force and direct financial aid to the new UHF stations. Another supporter, the distributors of TV films, National Telefilm Associates, furnished its library to UHF operators on time-payment plans (1955d). The unfair competition between UHF independents and VHF affiliates led 35 UHF stations to petition the FCC to restrict five cities to UHF-only, but the request was turned down (1955c). Under accusations of favoring the networks, the FCC started a deintermixture plan in March 1957 (Foster, 1982). The plan at that time was to take VHF out of eight medium-sized cities where UHF was working; push the all channel TV sets bill; and make UHF stations easier to get and build, by changing the standards for some of the equipment (1961).

According to Foster, "only one active VHF station was deleted. There were a handful of other markets that were deintermixtured but none of them had included VHF assignments in use" (Foster, 1982). Even though a real deintermixture (separation) between UHF and VHF stations never occurred, the plan touched for the first time on the major problem of the UHF introduction. Since there were few TV sets capable of tuning UHF, the advertisers were not attracted, and since there was less advertising money, the programming was less attractive and—closing the vicious cycle—viewers were not motivated to buy the more expensive UHF TV sets (1955c). Forcing all manufacturers to produce sets designed to tune both bands, the FCC expected to break the cycle and boost UHF development. Once again, there was a rush for new UHF licenses. In spite of warnings by the FCC that prolonged losses should be expected, 86 commercial stations plus 64 construction permits were quickly granted. For the first time, too, the FCC had contests between broadcasters wanting the same UHF assignment (1962a). But once again the stations failed to achieve profits. For each VHF station with financial problems, six UHF stations were calculated to have turned their licenses back to the FCC (1955e). The successive frustrations with the UHF enterprises called for many viability studies.

In October 1978, a definitive diagnosis of the so-called UHF handicap was produced through a national survey conducted by the UHF Comparability Task Force within the FCC. Among its many findings, the Task Force concluded that the main reasons generally accepted for the slow progress of the UHF stations were the higher costs of operation, poorer signal reception, tuning difficulties, and even poor programming (Boyle, 1980). The importance of such analyses to the flourish of UHF stations in Brazil in the late 1990s was in the definition of which problems the Brazilian enterprises were to expect and which were specific to the American pioneers. Following is a review of each of these challenges.

CHALLENGE 1: Higher Operational Costs

The upper position of UHF in the spectrum implies that much more energy is required to generate the wave signals, which usually have a shorter range—30 to 40 miles, compared with 50 to 60 for VHF (1964). For station managers, this means twice as much power is required to obtain the same coverage area as a VHF station. For engineer Bill Tessman, of Lansing's channel 47, the slower evolution of UHF technology is a direct consequence of its late start. The inefficiency of such amplifying devices was still great, however, in comparison to VHF. The early UHF amplifiers were only 30 percent efficient, and the four-feet-tall, 400-pounds tubes dissipated most of their energy as heat, requiring complex water cooling installations. In contrast, with efficiency rates reaching up to 90 percent, the VHF tubes needed less energy—about 5,000 volts—so can be smaller and air cooled. In 1966 the cost of operating a UHF station was estimated at between $500,000 and $1 million a year, plus a minimum of about $1 million to set it up (1966). About 30 years later, the efficiency was raised to figures between 50 and 60 percent, but Tessman reminds us that the cost of the sizable infrastructure required to manage energy supplies of around 25,000 volts and to cool the water from the amplifier refrigeration system remained two or three times that of a VHF competitor. Nevertheless, he believes that the UHF evolution was gradually being won on small grounds, and a transistorized UHF transmitter was expected by the end of the century. One of the simplest evolutions, he suggests, was the adoption of wave guides to deliver the signals from the studio to the transmitter tower. The wave guides substituted the coaxial cables with advantages and constituted square ducts where the radio waves bounce up to the sides, reflecting their way up to the top (Tessman, 1992). Until more efficient hardware could be developed, however, this overall technical handicap persisted for all UHF stations across the world.

CHALLENGE 2: Poorer Signal Reception

The physics of radio wave propagation also dictate unique patterns of signal transmission and interference by other sources of waves. While the VHF band is said to be more subject to interference from man-originated noises, like those coming from car ignition systems, neon signs or electrical machinery, UHF was once said to be more easily blocked by buildings and even trees (1951), ricocheting off the ground and metal surfaces (Benrey, 1964). In fact, the laws of physics do determine that the higher the frequency, the smaller the wave length and the easier the blockage. But the performance of UHF stations had to be repeatedly tested, with many contradictory results, before a virtual handicap of the higher frequencies could be forgotten. WUHF, channel 31 of New York proved that UHF would work in a large city, where the tall buildings could block the UHF signals (1961). Other tests indicated that UHF transmissions seemed better at night and in hot humid climates (Hertzberg, 1954). Overall, the picture quality of both frequencies ranges was found not to vary significantly and it is not an important issue today. The FCC Task Force produced revealing data about it:

> Most Americans find picture quality better on VHF channels than on UHF. However, there is no real difference between UHF and VHF channels in the comparative incidence of most reception problems. Weak signal or snow is more likely to be a problem on UHF than VHF channels. Nevertheless, this can hardly be the source of the perceived UHF picture quality handicap, since the difference in the incidence of snow is only pronounced among those who receive equal numbers of UHF and VHF channels... The survey finds, however, that less than half of the public (49%) receive at least one UHF channel whose picture quality they rate as excellent. Moreover, fully two thirds of the sample (66%) received more VHF than UHF stations with picture quality rated as good or excellent. Hence, the negative evaluation of UHF picture quality ... may have more to do with the availability of UHF reception than specific reception problems (p.97).

In essence, their conclusion was that the lower reach of UHF signals was responsible for a generalized negative perception, even though the picture quality is comparable within the more restricted coverage area. The signal propagation curves were based on statistical calculations, which were never really adapted from the American model to the Brazilian scenario. The temperatures, the landscape and the grounds are different, and the model is not perfect. In a skyscraper in a metropolis the delivery of any airwaves can be problematic, and in São Paulo the new UHF stations are facing very congested airwave traffic. Since the receiving antennas are not easily redirected, the stations tend to place their antennas in the same direction as the pioneer or most-watched channel. The Sumaré neighborhood, one of the highest points of São Paulo, has four TV transmission antennas— SBT, Manchete, Abril and Cultura. The Avenida Paulista antennas (Globo, Record and Gazeta) are not far away, causing all sorts of interference problems in radios, TVs, telephones and even medical equipment operating in the area. The concentration of powerful transmitters in one area makes the level of signals transmitted very high and, as these signals travel through the air, telephones and other equipment that generate electromagnetic fields can become reception antennas to them (Abreu, 1990). Unfortunately, the concessions to build antennas were given by the federal government and the city had no authority over them. The only valid municipal legislation is the Code of Buildings, which determines that any tower in town must be distanced from the sidewalk an equivalent of a fifth of its height (Abreu, 1990). Nevertheless, as the control is deficient, the majority of antennas were irregularly built and, if many have already received amnesty, others were getting regular penalty fees even as late as the mid 90s. The ideal solution would be to have all transmitters in one unique antenna, as has been done in Brasilia and many cities across the world.

The stations, however, never came to such an agreement, which requires all transmitters to have the same power and reach, whereas some companies wanted stronger transmitters (Mawakdye, 1992). Since the exposure to excessive radio and TV waves can cause damage to the human nervous system and reproductive organs, the state government ordered in January 1992 a report from the Institute of Electro-technique and Energy of the University of São Paulo. A previous study by Companhia deTecnologia e Saneamento Ambiental (Cetesb) in 1986, when there were fewer than a dozen antennas in the Avenida Paulista region, indicated radiation three times the limit imposed in America. In the mid-90s, there were 30 transmitter antennas and 2.8 million watts of power irradiated in the area, and concerned politicians were said to be elaborating a legal project to avoid more antenna concentrations like this (Mawakdye, 1992). The creation of UHF channels in all-VHF markets such as the Brazilian capitals demanded a few adaptations in the reception hardware, too. The television sets must be able to tune UHF channels, and the appropriate antennas must be installed. (Many issues of Popular Science magazine and others in the early fifties described the various newly designed UHF antennas: parabolic, rhombic, stacked vee, bow tie, etc.(1951).) Thus, the lack of UHF antennas can also be a problem associated with poorer signal reception, even though the FCC Task Force discarded the relevance of it:

> The impact of UHF antenna systems on the UHF reception handicap is relatively marginal .... Moreover, even with a UHF outdoor antenna, we find that a very formidable UHF reception handicap continues to exist .... However, the presence of some kind of UHF antenna significantly increases the number of UHF channels and the quality of reception on those stations .... It is important to note that lack of reception equipment does not make either UHF reception or UHF viewing impossible in some situations. Among those who have no UHF antenna on their primary television receiver, 62% report receiving one or more UHF channel, 36% report receiving one or more UHF channel with good or excellent picture quality, and 11% report some UHF viewing on the previous day. In each case, these rates are below those of individuals with indoor or outdoor UHF antennas (p. 101).

In Brazil, as shall be described in the following section, dealing about STV, the majority of external antennas used are old and scarcely effective. In a city full of buildings like São Paulo, most of the collective antennas work with VHF only. As a general rule, the smaller towns, which had already UHF retransmitters, seemed to be better prepared to receive these signals than the capitals, where the UHF had just made its debut in the early 90s. The new stations in São Paulo, on the other hand, have enhanced their transmissions with NTSC productions and stereo broadcasting. The stereo transmission enables the audience to listen to the dubbed or the original sound,

73

depending on the characteristics of the receiver. The new Brazilian TV sets included a feature called SAP (Second Audio Channel), which allows the choice of sound tracks to be received. Both Jovem Pan and MTV also operated internally with the American NTSC signals. The need for various transcoding between incompatible machines had been a common problem to television producers in Brazil, resulting in lower picture quality. On the other hand, they remained able to incorporate— faster and more efficiently—any technological development offered by the American and Japanese markets, which use the NTSC system and consist the main innovators in the industry. The conversion to the PAL-M system used in Brazil takes place only before broadcasting, in compliance to national telecommunications rules that prohibit television transmissions in systems other than PAL-M.

CHALLENGE 3: Tuning Difficulties

Probably the biggest disadvantage of the UHF late adoption was the lack of television sets capable of receiving the higher frequencies. Foster comments:

> If the Freeze had ended in 1948 rather than 1952, the UHF problem might not have developed to any significant degree. There were, at the earlier date, only fifty stations on the air and fewer than a million receivers in the country. When families bought television sets for the first time, it would have been much easier to persuade them to pay extra for a built-in UHF tuner and to put up antennas that were appropriate to the UHF signals as well as to the VHF. In many markets the UHF stations would have been minimal (Foster, 1982, p.135).

While there were an estimated 26 million VHF sets in America, only 2 to 3 million could tune UHF signals in the early 50s (1954a). Right after the introduction of the higher band, most manufacturers made experimental attachments to allow the UHF reception. The trick was to change the UHF to a VHF frequency not used for any channel (1951). But the costs involved were high, and there were just not enough UHF stations or desired programming to justify them. The cost of conversion to UHF was estimated at $40, including the converter and the labor of a new antenna installation—quite a lot for that time (1962b). Moreover, the UHF tuners had no pre-set channel buttons and required a patient and manual search for the best tuning position. The Task Force concluded:

> Today (1980), UHF channels suffer a serious disadvantage in ease of tuning. Only one third of the public (33%) find that there is no difference in ease of tuning. Nearly half (47%) feel that it is easier to tune VHF channels, while only 3% find it easier to tune UHF... The principal criticism of current mechanical systems of channel selection is that they require more effort to turn channels among the highly dispersed UHF channels, than to select the highly clustered VHF channels.... This tuning handicap does have a significant relationship with viewership. Only 14% of those who find it easier to tune VHF channels on their television watched any UHF television on the day before the interview. By contrast, 26% of those who find no difference in channel tuning had watched some UHF television, while 52% of those who find it easier to tune UHF report UHF viewing (p. 128).

This vicious cycle was only broken ten years after the end of the Freeze, with "an amendment to the Communications Act, allowing the FCC to require that all television sets sold in interstate commerce include a UHF tuner" (Foster, 1982). At that point, an alarming 50 out of 55 million sets received only VHF signals (1962b). And, in spite of the compliance deadline of 1964, the fear of losing buyers with a $20 price increase kept the production of new sets at a slow pace. Less than one year before the deadline, only 20 percent of TV sets produced were all-channel receivers (1963). In the following years, as manufacturers increased production, the new sets started coming out of the factories with built-in UHF tuners (See Table 5), the transistors previously adapted only for those tuners gradually became generalized to the whole set.

Modern electronic television receivers have made all channels equally easy to tune, so this challenge is not significant in America anymore. Nevertheless, the new Brazilian UHF stations were facing similar problems in the early 90s, especially in the capitals, where UHF was just starting. Three decades after the American all-channels law and the introduction of television in Brazil, a 1982 law required the

Brazilian sets to offer UHF tuning (Pinto, 1982). But it was generally estimated that the majority of the 3.8 million TV households in Brazil had sets unable to receive UHF signals. The all-channel receivers have practically arrived in the Brazilian market only in 1989 and alternative tuning devices were still in demand.

Table 5 - U.S. TV sets versus UHF/VHF stations (1958-1990)

Year	Stations	VHF	UHF	Units	Dollars
1958				5,131	720,000
1959				6,368	843,000
1960	515	440	75	5,829	797,000
1961				6,315	814,000
1962				7,134	1,005,000
1963				7,983	1,099,000
1964				9,764	1,384,000
1965	569	481	88	11,477	1,869,000
1966				12,714	2,617,000
1967				11,564	2,570,000
1968				13,211	2,677,000
1969				13,308	2,585,000
1970	677	501	176	12,220	2,202,000
1971				14,921	2,976,000
1972				17,084	3,474,000
1973				17,368	3,657,000
1974				15,279	3,201,000
1975	706	514	192	10,637	2,492,000
1976				14,131	3,388,000
1977				15,431	3,811,000
1978				17,407	4,308,000
1979				16,617	4,180,000
1980	734	516	218	18,532	4,939,000
1981				17,423	4,854,000
1982				17,365	4,760,000
1983				20,045	5,467,000
1984				21,613	5,957,000

Year	Stations	VHF	UHF	Units	Dollars
1985	883	520	363	20,829	5,872,000
1986				22,721	6,353,000
1987				23.300	6,559,000
1988				23,460	6,253,000
1989	1064	545	519	24,669	6,900,000
1990	1186	569	617	23,065	6,624,000

Source: Broadcasting & Cable Market 1992. Data compiled by Electronic Industries Association. TV sets figures are in thousands. Television & Video Almanac 1992 - 37th. Edition.

Since VCRs could tune UHF channels, they became important allies. The companies emphasized the better reception of their broadcast signals by stressing all possible tuning methods in their promotional campaigns. The impact of tuning difficulties on new segmented UHF stations like MTV-Abril or Jovem Pan was not likely to be very significant, though. Their target markets consisted of higher classes, which counted on newer all-channel TV sets or any other tuning device. But among the four million TV households in metro São Paulo, for example, only 1.5 million could receive UHF signals (1990h). TV Abril calculated that 1,290,000 households had TV sets and/or VCRs able to receive UHF signals in São Paulo. This 30 percent of total households was raised to 57 percent within class B; 84 percent within class A (Department, 1990).

The penetration among the higher classes was also facilitated by satellite relay and VCR tuning. It was estimated that there were more than 150,000 parabolic antennas and between 800,000 and 1 million VCRs in Brazil, which meant the same number of potential UHF receivers (Luiz, 1989) (Department, 1990). Like the FCC did just before the implementation of the all-channel law, the UHF stations of São Paulo launched a joint campaign in February 1991 to teach the public the various ways to capture the UHF transmissions. Using basically in-house resources, the campaign involved Jovem Pan radio, Abril magazines and millions of pamphlets distributed across the city. For young audiences like MTV's, the campaign was more effective.

Abril officials explain that the youngsters were more curious and more knowledgeable about electronic equipment, having fewer difficulties setting up the TV receivers.

CHALLENGE 4: Bad Programming

The UHF Comparability Task Force found basic programming deficiencies with UHF broadcasting:

> Since public preference for network programming has been repeatedly demonstrated by audience share studies, the limited access to network programming—only 20% of American communities have any UHF channel that serves as a primary network affiliate—represents a fundamental handicap to UHF broadcasting. A full third of the viewing public report that none of the programs they enjoy are carried on local UHF channels. Moreover, since UHF stations generally have smaller audiences and revenues, it should be more difficult to produce or purchase programming (p.133).

That was a time when UHF was synonymous with independent station and poor or alternative programming. For the young Brazilian enterprises, the survival of UHF stations with segmented programming, especially those targeting ethnic groups or the public affairs of local communities, otherwise represented a positive sign. Chicago's WCIU was proof that local UHF stations connected to the community had a chance to survive. Its programming was based on taped soccer games, wrestling, bullfights, and performances by local ethnic groups (1964). These stations found original programming suitable for their focused markets and survived with less audience shares. As Chapter 5 points out, the original programming offered by the segmented stations in São Paulo had interested market niches as well. In the search for programming that would attract audience and advertisers, many UHF stations opted in the 1960s to eliminate advertisers and become subscription channels (STV). That was the case of WBSX, channel 31 of Ann Arbor, Michigan. President Christopher J. Webb explained that, as the station found itself with financial problems, it scrambled the signals and became an STV channel, but with the arrival of cable television the station opened the transmissions again. In the early

90s, WBSX was a full-time affiliate of Home Shopping Network, broadcasting direct sales programming and enjoying a performance evaluation based on sales instead of ratings (Webb, 1992).

But the real change in this scenario came only in 1988, when Fox Broadcasting Co. launched its new network. Producing and/or syndicating shows aimed at younger audiences, Fox started with shows that aired one night a week through a chain of 105 independent stations, most of them UHF. Beating all the challenges of UHF, Fox offered alternative programming for an audience that was not totally satisfied with the family entertainment proposed by the Big Three networks. The so-called "baby boomers" (18 to 49 year-olds) were the right target, with money and a desire to spend it. The advertisers, on the other hand, were happy with prices that were half of those charged by other networks. Behind this winning strategy was Barry Diller, the former Fox Chairman who was also responsible for ABC's jump from the third to the first place in the mid-1970s. With marketing strategies that included the broadcasting of original episodes in the summer, when the audiences are smaller and networks usually offer reruns, Fox overcame losses of $50 million in 1987 and by the mid 1990s was filling almost five nights of the week with audience shares that threatened—and eventually beat—the networks (Grover, 1987).

CHALLENGE 5: Measurability?

A fifth challenge in Brazil was associated with the lack of ratings for UHF stations. Even though they offered good programming and were attracting significant audiences, the UHF broadcasters found it difficult to attract advertisers without a measure of their market penetration. In their early days, indexes were substituted by the prestige of the parent companies, but magical numbers were soon demanded. Without an audience index in São Paulo, Abril used the phone calls received by its "Disk MTV" program to evaluate the reception by the public (Flesch, 1990).

Others were simply relying on the work of advertising agencies. The media departments of advertising agencies worked with information furnished by the stations, in the same manner as they used to do for magazines before the Instituto de Veiculação Comercial (IVC) started doing regular measurements about the printed media (Luiz, 1989). By mid-1991, Instituto Brasileiro de Opinião Pública e Estatística (IBOPE), one of the most respected market research companies in Brazil, experimentally included some UHF channels in its periodical audience report, more specifically for channels 32 (MTV) and 16 (Jovem Pan).

The bulk of the reports was based on the People Meter survey system, which had electronic devices connected to the main TV set of 256 households in metro São Paulo (See Table 6). The devices indicate the channel tuned at every moment, including the time the VCRs are used, but contains a major flaw. It could not indicate the use of VCRs to tune UHF channels, a practice considered common among the middle class, which owns older TV sets connected to VCRs. Thus, the solution adopted was to add an approximate 20 percent of the VCR viewership to the audience of each UHF channel. Moreover, IBOPE calculated that only 37 percent of the surveyed households were capable of receiving UHF signals, which put under suspicion the statistical validity of the data. As the audience shares rarely exceeded one percent or approximately 37,000 families in São Paulo, the margin of error was quite considerable (Lima, 1992).

Table 6 - Brazilian IBOPE People Meter ratings of MTV

Date/hour	Sets on	VHF	UHF	JP	MTV	Others	VCR
1/25/92							
10h30	19.09	17.80	0.09	0.03	0.06	-	1.21
14h00	37.87	34.78	0.15	0.09	0.06	-	2.96
18h00	46.50	43.64	0.71	0.71	-	-	2.53
20h00	52.08	49.05	0.76	0.76	-	-	2.28
1/26/92							
10h30	22.51	21.26	-	-	-	-	1.26
14h00	40.58	36.56	0.86	-	0.46	0.40	3.17
18h00	46.74	43.63	0.03	-	0.03	-	4.00

Date/ hour	Sets on	VHF	UHF	JP	MTV	Others	VCR
20h00	55.76	51.56	0.30	0.03	0.27	-	3.92
1/27/92							
10h30	23.56	21.79	-	-	-	-	1.77
14h00	45.76	43.73	-	-	-	-	2.40
18h00	44.64	43.32	0.49	-	0.49	-	1.01
20h00	65.64	62.98	0.29	0.23	0.03	0.03	2.83
1/30/92							
10h30	21.15	20.84	0.07	-	0.07	-	0.25
14h00	43.95	42.23	0.03	0.03	-	-	2.15
18h00	52.06	48.92	0.48	0.45	-	0.03	2.68
20h00	71.17	67.94	1.12	0.42	0.62	0.09	2.74

Note: Survey based on Metro São Paulo universe of 3,979,000 television sets.

4.1.3 UHF Today (by mid-90s anyway!)

Most of the UHF problems had been overcome by the mid-90s (when this study was conducted) and the number of UHF stations had actually surpassed the VHF stations (See Table 5 previously). The percentage of profitable UHF stations increased from 37 in 1967 to 58 in 1980, and no UHF station had gone off the air since 1976 (1969b) (1982c). For many professionals, the growth of UHF was greatly boosted by the concomitant penetration of cable television in America. Arriving at the subscribers' TV sets with equally good picture quality and tuning ease, VHF and UHF channels could hardly be distinguished anymore. But the development of cable was withheld by the FCC, especially in the larger cities (top 100 markets), due to fears that cable's distant signal importation would be fatal to the weaker UHF independents.

The 1970 Rand Report concluded, however, that "the effect of cable was to increase the revenues of UHF independent stations in the near term (through the 1970s), and decrease them in later years.

UHF independents generally got larger audience shares on the cable in competition with distant signals than they did over the air in homes with UHF sets" (Park, 1970). Since the UHF entrants in São Paulo were leasing satellite transponders to deliver signals to affiliates all over the country, the growth of cable in Brazil was also positive, as a possible alternative outlet. In 1992, the FCC authorized American networks to have "cable affiliates" where their programming cannot be provided by a local station. This was to become a better solution in Brazil.

According to engineer Lucrécia Costa of TV Jovem Pan, the São Paulo UHF stations were facing many problems to enlist affiliates in the 1990s. In some areas, it was virtually impossible to add another UHF channel because of bad or irresponsible transmission setups. She explained that the intercity relays that should use focused transmissions, usually irradiated signals in a large area, affecting nearby stations. Since there was no rule concerning the technical standards for retransmission, a better use of the airwaves could hardly be enforced. Moreover, in the smaller cities, where the local government owns the satellite dishes that bring all the channels to town, the decision to rebroadcast another channel can be a political one. MTV and Jovem Pan were the main competitors in these markets and, while the mayor's kids may be pressuring him for MTV, Pan is marketing its news service as political-plus, similar to the way CNN did among cable operators. Worsening the situation, explained Lucrécia, were equipment manufacturers that approached prospective affiliates and sold inadequate equipment. Most parabolic antennas in use across the country were not able to receive the signals of a half transponder, which requires high-power receivers and larger antennas (Costa, 1992).

As a result of the 1980 UHF Comparability Task Force, the FCC decided not to do anything else to help UHF other than explain to consumers how they could enhance the broadcasted UHF images by installing proper antenna systems. At the same time, the FCC also abolished a rule requiring TV set manufacturers to include channels 70 to 83, which had already been used by land mobile radio services, a market that grew from $7 to $20 million between 1958 and 1968 (1959) (1982c).

In fact, the success of many UHF stations did not mean a more comprehensive use of this portion of the spectrum, and other radio services started taking a bite off the UHF band. Scientists requested it for the study of the cosmos and, in more than thirteen American markets, private land mobile radio services shared channels 14 to 20 with television (1986). In Brazil, the UHF channels 74 to 78 had also been conquered by the growing mobile telephony services, a market estimated at $2 billion at the time (1991j). But the biggest bite was soon to come, with the High Definition Television (HDTV). Initially using more than twice the 6 MHz used by the standard television channels, HDTV was expected to take a large portion of the spectrum. Bill Tessman, from Lansing's channel 47 saw a future where each station received an extra channel and most of the operations moved to the wider UHF band, leaving VHF for other services. This kind of forecast, however, may only be a revival of controversial arguments in the late 1950s in favor of an all-UHF television. In 1959, the FCC believed that 50 contiguous channels were needed to provide adequate TV service for five stations in each of the 100 largest American cities, and FCC Commissioner Robert E. Lee favored scrapping the VHF structure and moving all television to UHF (1959). With the multiplication of radio services, the battle for the finite spectrum was likely to grow—but little did anyone know what the digital transition of the 21st Century was to bring.

4.2 STV, MDS, MMDS and the like

The concept of a television system paid for by the viewers instead of advertisers is almost as old as television itself. But there have always been ethical and technical difficulties associated with pay-TV systems. There is a need to convince viewers to pay for what is customarily free and, at the same time, find technology that efficiently and cheaply restricts the signals to subscribers only. In 1951, three American companies were thought to have the answers. Zenith was authorized to test its Phonevision system in Chicago, followed in 1954 by Skiatron in New York City, and Paramount Pictures' Telemeter in Palm Springs. They transmitted scrambled signals and devised three different systems for the viewers to pay for certain television programs: dropping coins or inserting a computer card into a meter attached to the TV set, calling the telephone company, or flipping a switch connected to a telephone cable wired to the set (1955a).

In any case, these pioneer experiences enjoyed some relative success and attracted the networks' attention. The networks feared the challengers' proposed plans to produce TV shows and sell to local TV stations, sharing with them the money taken in from the subscribers who view each show (1955b). The debate promoted at that time by the media was whether fee TV was broadcasting—since it involved subscription and the use of extra equipment—and whether it was legal to charge people for programming sent over "free" public air (1955a). On the last week of February 1958, the Senate Commerce Committee asked the FCC to hold up pay-TV tests pending a decision by Congress on the whole issue. This killed the possibility of pay-TV tests already authorized by FCC and postponed over-the-air pay-TV indefinitely. In the meantime, wired pay-TV, which did not need FCC authorization, was having difficulties. Bartlesville, Oklahoma, the only operating commercial plant, was forced to reduce programming and monthly charges to attract subscribers. In Los Angeles, two other plants returned franchises to the city a few months after they were granted, due to fears of an uncertain government policy on the future of the industry (1958) .

Bartlesville lost a reported $500,000 when it closed in 1958; and Subscription TV, Inc. went bankrupt in Los Angeles after a few months of operation in 1954, losing $26 million (1968). Not all networks boycotted pay-TV, though. CBS even considered that it could make more money than it was making by using pay-TV. A survey CBS conducted in Columbus, Ohio showed that 25 percent of the TV audience would be willing to pay to see some shows, under what CBS called ,"optimum conditions" (1955b). CBS even found that 70 percent of American top advertisers were in favor of "toll-TV" (1956). It was never successful, however, in garnering a significant return on the investments. A decade-long history of abortive trials and power lobbying by both sides kept pay-TV in the news, but out of the market.

The pressure on Congress was so high that it twice rejected FCC proposals for a test run of pay-TV—first in 1957 and again in 1958. In 1959, a sum of circumstances allowed it another chance. The networks were still suffering the effects of the so-called "plugola" scandal[5] and were not in position to attack the competitors. And since the FCC was considering authorizing subscription privileges to FM stations, the equally troubled UHF stations should receive the same treatment (1955a). Congress finally accepted the FCC's trial with three conditions: the test was to be restricted to one area, with three free programming stations, and the results of the three-year period would be reported to Congress. This approval was a result of the FCC's chairman Frederick Ford's policy to start pay-TV over the air before it would go by wire, a system not controlled by the FCC at the time and which Paramount Pictures was promising to develop across America (1960).

The company that was awarded this new trial, RKO-Zenith, selected a UHF station with the hope that the need and cost of a converter would filter out viewers with insufficient interest in TV (or money) to pay for a converter. Moreover, there were fewer applications for UHF than VHF, making the proposal more likely to be accepted. Channel 18 of Hartford, Connecticut, was a hybrid, with 28 hours of pay-TV during primetime and free programming during the rest of the day. It broadcast four hours of pay-TV each night for 5,500 subscribers out of 275,000 TV homes covered by the station's signal. While it was successful in getting recent movies, it could not get specials or sports events of high cost (1968). In the application, RKO compromised by agreeing not to transmit any sports events that were shown free on TV (1960). Mindful that complaints would be strong if sets conked out during a subscription show, installation crews rejected about 15 percent of the applications (1962c). RKO expected to invest $10 million during the three years and get 5,000 subscribers by 1963, but to turn a profit it would need around 50,000 subscribers, each paying out an average of $1.50 per week for programs (1962c).

---

5 The law prohibits the advertisement of certain activities, without the public being aware that such material is being broadcast for pay (plugola).

By the end of the three-year experiment, pay-TV accumulated losses of $12 million.

The House Committee on Interstate & Foreign Commerce and the FCC, which had battled for the right to authorize pay-TV on a national scale, were then advised to do nothing for a year while the situation was studied (1968). In fact, pay television was still a controversial idea. Against pay-TV were the networks (NAB), the Theater Owners Association, and even a Connecticut Committee Against pay TV, a group composed of veterans, women and civil groups (1960). The brochure, "Does the American family need another mouth to feed?," signed by Arthur R. Taylor for CBS, comments:

> The basic notion of pay cable television ... is nothing more than that the average television viewer should pay for the programs that he now receives free. The effect of this change in the free broadcasting industry would be an incalculable disservice to the American viewing public (Taylor, 1975, p.330). But the RKO-Zenith concept of a UHF pay-TV system caught on, and when the FCC authorized the subscription television service (STV) in 1968, that concept was adopted—along with all the restrictions that blocked its growth. The so-called "antisiphoning rules," which precluded STV from most sports events and movies launched before two to ten years pleased broadcasters and theatre owners, but kept STV from any valuable programming. The restriction to markets with four conventional stations and the technical difficulties of charging for individual problems did not help either. In the 1970s, the STV enjoyed a relative success with the end of restrictive laws, concerning the programming and the markets, respectively, in 1977 and 1979. As Foster describes, Wometco Horne Theater in 1977 became the first successful STV operation in New York City. Three years later there were eight stations—all on the UHF band—with over 400,000 subscribers. Each was offering an STV service with monthly charges about $20. Typical scheduling included fifty hours "a week composed of domestic and foreign movies (unedited and uninterrupted by commercials), sports, events, and occasional specials (Foster, 1982, p.135).

It is noteworthy that this new batch of pay-tv services was sold by the month rather than by individual programs. And, together with the fact that many UHF stations were still having financial problems at the time, a favorable environment appeared for STV. In the early 1980s, some 1.5 million Americans subscribed (Barbieri, 1985). But the circumstances quickly changed with the expansion of the competing cable systems and the increased commercial value of UHF stations. STV was a more efficient system than cable, presenting advantages like ease of installation, technical viability in areas of different population densities, and a much smaller operational cost. However, cable's higher quality of signals and channel capacity for similar prices represented a stronger appeal (Hoineff, 1991). STV companies felt they could find a niche in cities not served by cable, but as cable increased its penetration toward the 60 percent, co-existence became impossible. It had been calculated that up to 90 percent of STV subscribers discontinued such service when a cable company started operating in the same area (Hoineff, 1991). Sensing the rising prospects for UHF stations as advertising-supported media, some broadcasters, which used to lease time to STV operators, also started to refuse to expand STV hours, at the same time increasing prices considerably (1983c).

Thus, by 1983 the STV was in frank decline in America, while it had not even started in Brazil (Hoineff, 1991). As the subscriber base dropped to 1.1 million, from a peak of 1.4 million on July 1982, 65,000 subscribers became necessary to break-even, compared to 47,000 two years before (1983c). The president of channel 31 of Ann Arbor, Michigan, Christopher J. Webb, says that the decision to terminate STV services was usually based on the difficulty of making customers pay the bills, while many were pirating the signal with illegal decoder boxes sold by other bankrupted services. The numbers of the decadence were impressive. OAK Industries, Inc., a giant STV operator, with 17,400 STV subscribers in Dallas and 31,700 in Phoenix, shut down both services after losing 45 percent and 37 percent of their respective subscriber base (1983c). After a year of service, Cox Communications Inc. closed operations in St. Louis (1983c). In 1984, the situation became critical. Not a single major STV operation had started in more than two years, while fifteen services closed and the total number of subscribers had dropped to less than half of STV's peak (Goldstein, 1984). By 1985 even STV's trade association had closed its doors. The Chicago, Cincinnati and Miami STV stations closed, leaving New York, Los Angeles and Washington as the only big cities with STV service. The nationwide subscribership was under 300,000 and in only one trimester this figure dropped 100,000 (Barbieri, 1985).

4.2.1 Higher frequencies, more television

Delivering more than one channel or operating as a common carrier, other paid broadcasting services created in the 1970s were expected to have a better fate. Generally called wireless cable, in reference to cable's multichannel capacity, these services broadcast omnidirectional microwave (2 GHz) signals to subscribers at line of sight within an average of 25 miles. The subscribers need special rooftop antennas, descramblers and a downconverter. The initial assignment of 31 such channels in each market was aimed at benefitting "nonprofit groups interested in broadcasting instructional programming," but these groups never managed to effectively use services like the ITFS (Instructional Television Fixed Service) or OFS (Operational Fixed Service). Thus in 1969, when it started to face a shrinking interest for its low-cost closed circuit TV equipment to the education market, Varian Associates, of Palo Alto, California, pioneered the so-called MDS (Multipoint Distribution Service). With Lipper's Microband Corp. of America, it planned to sell time on an MDS network to pharmaceutical companies aiming at doctors in hospitals, car manufacturers aiming at their dealers, and even companies that would transmit movies to hotel guests. The FCC's ruling of MDS as a common carrier in 1970 opened it in 180 cities and the 350 applicants for the individual channels spent about $1,000 for antenna dishes to send messages to stores and affiliates around the city, like management reports, new product presentations, etc. (1973).

In May 1983, the FCC allowed schools to lease time on their ITFS channels to commercial firms, provided that at least three hours per weekday is used for actual education. This made some ITFS operations economically viable and greatly increased the use of commercial MOS. But, in the end, 8 of the 28 ITFS channels were lost in cities where they had not already been claimed, and the MOS boom quickly vanished. From 750,000 in 1982, the total MDS subscribership decreased to some 500,000 in 1984. With more channels available, the single channel MDS became a multichannel service. This variation of the MDS service appeared in 1982, when Staggs Telecommunication Services successfully operated eight transmitters of eight consecutive channels in Salt Lake City (Hoineff, 1991). The MMOS (Multichannel Multipoint Distribution Service) was expected to succeed at cities without cable. The capital required to start an MMDS system is smaller than for cable. Big city cable franchisees were faced with up-front construction costs of as much as $1,400 per eventual subscriber, while MMDS needed to invest only $300 per subscriber, and then only after signing him up. Some 16,000 applications for four-channel MMDS licenses were pending in the fall of 1984 at the FCC, awaiting selection by lottery. "According to the Wireless Cable Association, some tk systems served more than 300,000 subscribers in the U.S. in 1991" (Yuster, 1992).

4.2.2 Will pay-TV work in Brazil?

The concept of pay-TV arrived in Brazil in similar modes. The less costly infrastructures of wireless systems enjoyed a quicker development and more legal support than cable communications. And the acceptance of high fees was not a problem among the reasonably large number of elites in the capital cities, most of whom were acquainted with the pay-TV concept (see subscription sales in Chapter 5). In 1982, a decree first identified STV as a special service under the radio-difusion regulations (Pinto, 1982). But it was only in 1988 that President José Sarney created subscription TV through a decree in the Union Official Diary of February 23rd. STV programming could include advertising (up to 10 minutes per hour) and it was not subject to any kind of censorship. STV could follow the same legislation that applied to regular television in what concerns the concession period for it (15 years, renewable for an equal period) and the prohibitions on it (it was not allowed to incite civil disobedience, propagate contraventions or facts that are anti-moralist, among others). The licensees were required to be native Brazilians and could not transfer concessions within five years of the granting (1988c). On other points, however, STV followed different rules. The regular TV networks, for example, were free to explore the service, and like the regulation of FM radios, STV could not be transmitted in a national or regional network form (Mauad & Rocha Filho, 1990). As interested parties, the Brazilian networks did not boycott STV—at this point at least—like the American networks did in America. More important, the president could distribute STV concessions without approval from Congress. The legal basis for this was in article 81, item 111 of the Constitution and article 15 of the Norms for STV Special Service. These norms were instituted by decree number 95.744 and altered by decree number 95.815 of March 10, 1988 (Teixeira, 1988). The official notice number 90 of the Communication Ministry opened the competition for STV channels in the metro São Paulo area on March 24, 1988 and fourteen candidates applied: Pira Som & Imagem Ltda., TV Tres Ltda., Ipe Radio e Televisao Ltda., Radio Jornal de São Paulo Ltda., TV Manchete, Rede Jocam de Comunicação, Paulista Metro, TVA, Rede Jaraguá de Televisão, Casablanca Produções Cine VT, DVT Cine VT Produções , Art Studio Radiodifusão, TV SBT Canal 4 de São Paulo and Televisão Show Time.

Alleging technical reasons, the Communication Minister Antonio Carlos Magalhães changed the first concession, granted to Abril Publishing's TVA, from the planned channel 50 to 24, which benefitted Abril with a less interference-sensitive channel. Globo Network's Paulista Metro, Show Time (owned by Sarney's friend Mathias Machline) and the recently created Pira Som & Imagem were also awarded at that time. Within a year after that, the Communication Ministry had opened concessions in Rio de Janeiro, Vitória, Porto Alegre and Salvador. In 1990, president Sarney waited for the recess of the Legislative to distribute, at once, ten subscription television channels: four in Rio de Janeiro, two in Porto Alegre, two in Brasília, one in Fortaleza and one in Vitória. At Rio, where the official notice 255/88 had been receiving applications since August 5, 1989, the competitors for an estimated 500,000 subscribers were Globo' s Rio Metro, Machline's Show Time, Nova Comunicação (connected to Politician Álvaro Pacheco) and Rádio RPC FM (owned by Paulo Cesar Ferreira, connected to Globo's vice-president). In Porto Alegre Rede Brasil Sul (Globo affiliate) and São Paulo Enlaces (connected to Machline) have applied (Sá, 1990).

The avoidance of the Congress was granted by Justice Minister Saulo Ramos, who used a loophole in the constitutional norms to reassure, two months before, that the concession of subscription channels were to be the exclusive responsibility of the Executive power. The loophole was based this time on the definition of radio-diffusion. A 1962 law (number 4.117) stated that the radio-diffusion service was the one that distributes signals "in a direct and free manner." Paid television would be, therefore, a special service, not under Congressional supervision. However, even if this definition of radio-diffusion were to be accepted, another law of 1988 (number 95.744) allowed the "use of STV partially without coding"—w which makes it radio-diffusion service (Sá, 1990). In this first phase, the Communications Ministry gave STV concessions only to state capitals, leaving the medium-size cities to a second phase. Until the beginning of 1990, fourteen concessions had been distributed, not exceeding four in each city. São Paulo and Rio de Janeiro got four, Brasilia and Porto Alegre got two, Fortaleza and Vitória got one (Mauad & Rocha Filho, 1990).

The challenge of these channels was to conquer the majority of the Brazilian higher classes, a market relatively small, compared to the overall population. One STV channel risked calculating that there were two million prospective viewers of STV in Brazil. From these, 50 percent would be in São Paulo city, 20 percent in the interior of the state of São Paulo, and 30 percent spread all over the rest of the country (1991w). More conservative studies estimated the potential of STV as equivalent to 20 percent of sets turned off during the peak audience periods of the networks programming (1988e). In any case, more than enough to support a couple of STV channels. In May 1992, the companies in operation estimated that at least 70,000 subscribers paying between $20 and $40 on a monthly fee would be required for any of the operations to reach a break-even point (Iori, 1992). The limitation of the signal broadcast to the paying subscribers was done by scrambling the signals. In the UHF/STV system, the signals were available to anyone with a TV set that had the capacity to receive UHF channels. Images could only be descrambled at the viewer's home equipped with specific decoder equipment. The adoption of common decoder equipment by all companies was the first challenge faced by these fledgling competitors. The Communications Ministry repeatedly

91

stated that the national industry was capable of producing the decoders on a large scale and, indeed, there were a couple of plans in that respect. Machline, who also owned a group of electronics companies, stated that it would consider the manufacture of decoders in case the importation proved less interesting, and Abril planned to build a decoder factory, before the threat of competition made it abandon the idea (Picillo, 1989). The pioneer STV company in Brazil, Machline's Canal+, ended up importing the American Zenith sets, but the other stations did not approve of such choices.

A pool of companies—Metro Paulista, Alpha and Abril agreed to let the Brazilian Society of Engineering and Television (SET) evaluate the best equipment and suggest the standard for them. Thus, on September 12, 1989, SET promoted a conference in São Paulo, gathering large manufacturers of decoders for pay-tv systems, such as Phillips Brasil, Nozatek (Argentina), Scientific Atlanta, Zenith Electronic Co. and Comband (USA). Even though the choice of a decoder was not promptly achieved by SET, the conference produced interesting reports. Overall, the SET opinion elaborated that the viability of STV in Brazil would depend on the formation of networks, uniting several companies with one programming lineup. Only this way could the costs be reduced and the programming quality be maintained (1989c). On January 22, 1990, three new channels—all in the super high frequency (3 GHz to 30 GHz) band—were added to the Canal+ operations, making it the first MMDS system in Brazil. The SHF use, however, had not been regulated yet. According to Telecommunications consultant José Cappia, the Official Diary of January 3, 1991 launched a public consultation of decree 131 of December 11, 1990, but the proposed law remained unverified and unapproved (Cappia, 1992). The concern of engineer Lucrécia Costa, from Jovem Pan, was that the original proposal included the use of the two GHz frequency for MMDS, the same one used by television stations for the transmission of on-site news, electronic news gathering (ENG) (Costa, 1992).

The MMDS initial expansion was troubled by a less than enthusiastic reception of UHF and SHF by potential consumers. Some eight percent of the São Paulo residents interested in receiving UHF and STV channels did not receive quality, or strong, signals. For those receiving SHF signals, the proportion rose to 30 percent

(Delmanto, 1991). In June 1990, the 200 technicians .of TVA tackled the problem with 100 installation and repair crews that performed an average of 6,000 services a month. Newton Guerra, general director of TVA, confirmed at that time a number of about 100 customers with image problems and installation delay of five weeks. According to the Videotel Company, specialized in developing collective antenna systems, the antenna systems in buildings were capable of receiving only a dozen channels; furthermore, there was not a single building in São Paulo capable of receiving all of the 13 channels then available.

The problem was economic: a simple antenna could cost $20, 000, while an antenna for CATV (and the adequate cabling) would cost $80 to $100,000 in currency exchange of January 1992 (Magalhães, 1991). Videotel officers justify the high costs as the equivalent of building a vertical cable plant. At a time when cable was expanding not only in America, but in several countries, the wireless option demanded some more supporting arguments. The over-the-air system presented cheaper and easier implementation, making it more appropriate to the smaller size of Brazilian elite and the economic difficulties of the country. Those who defended the system mentioned the successful experience of STV in France, besides other Latin American countries. By 1983 Peru, Argentina and Bolivia already had American-like STV systems operating with legally questionable programming—retransmissions of American cable channels captured from the satellite (Hoineff, 1991). While the Brazilian pay-TV started as strictly legal in 1988, one of the first other legal services in South America appeared only in 1990. HBO and Omnivision, a Venezuelan subscription channel, created a Spanish-speaking movie channel—the HBO-Ole—transmitted via PanamSat to Latin America.

In the same period, the president of HBO International, Steve Rosenberg, announced his intention of creating a similar channel in Portuguese, aiming at the Brazilian market (Hoineff, 1991). This study speculated at the time that HBO could very well provide the programming that Globo's STV channels had been waiting for. In fact, the importation of programming by the Brazilian STV systems were expected to assure their survival even in a future where cable had become a significant competitor in the country. As it indeed happened, the STV operators morphed into programming providers to cable systems with the imported programming, whose exclusive rights they locally held, making use of the same satellite by which they originally planned to distribute their signals to various affiliates around the country.

4.3 Cable's Competitive Edge

The wonders of cable television—a television signal distribution system that delivered more than thirty channels with perfect picture quality at prices comparable to STV channels—have been held responsible for the decline of other pay-TV systems. But, before cable would dramatically expand in the 1980s to conquer 60 percent of the American households (See Table 7), the operators had to overcome serious problems. The laws did not favor cable expansion. There was a lack of desirable programming and the high investments were not compensated by public demand—a scenario not too different from, the situation of cable in Brazil circa 1993. Thus, the question many scholars and entrepreneurs were asking themselves was whether Brazilian cable systems could enjoy success some day.

Table 7 - American cable penetration increase

	Operating Systems	Subscribers (000)	% of TV Homes
1960	640	0.7	1.4
1965	1,325	1.3	2.4
1970	2,490	4.5	7.6
1975	3,366	9.8	14.3
1980	4,048	15.5	20.5
1985	6,600	37.3	43.7
1991	10,704	56.07	60.3

Source: National Cable Television Association, Warren Publishing & Nielsen Media Research. Reproduced from Television & Video Almanac 1992.

Although a different political set and a revitalized economy should precede the expansion of cable in Brazil, there were signs that indicated cable could make more sense in the following years. Most significantly, community antenna systems were multiplying in buildings and condominiums interested in tuning the STV and DBS services already offered (See Table 8). The old community antennas were being substituted by more sophisticated equipment, capable of receiving the multitude of channels presently available. And it was possible to foresee a day when cable would start to reach not only a building, but a whole neighborhood.

Table 8 - Cable Concessions in Brazil

Per State	
São Paulo	30
Rio Grande do Sul	23
Paraná	13
Santa Catarina	12
Minas Gerais	5
Ceará	2
Goiás	2
Mato Grosso do Sul	2
Rio de Janeiro	2
Bahia	1
Federal District	1
Maranhão	1
Per Year	
1987	1
1988	4
1989	11
1990	15

Source: Istoé/Senhor magazine. p. 19. 6/31/91. and TVCabo Ltda. 1/20/91

In fact, the origins of cable are associated with the creation of Community Antenna Television (CATV) systems to solve bad television signal reception. Between 1948 and 1949, entrepreneurs

95

like Ed Parsons of Astoria, Oregon, or John Walson of Mahanoy City and Robert J. Tarlton of Lansford, Pennsylvania, built master antennas over higher hills to capture distant signals, amplify them and deliver to some houses in the valleys through coaxial cables hung on poles. CATV grew because of the FCC freeze on new stations between September 30, 1948 and July 1, 1952, which limited the number of television stations to 108—not enough to cover the whole American territory. Meanwhile, the number of sets continued to increase, from 250,000 in 1948 to 15 million in 1952, and CATV became a solution to communities not served by any station. The end of the freeze did not limit CATV, as the first broadcasting stations were only built in large communities and many small towns were still not served. As Baldwin and McVoy describe:

> From 1949, the number of cable systems grew slowly but steadily. By 1961 there were 700 community antenna TV systems. Growth accelerated so that in 1971 there were 2,750 systems serving nearly six million homes entirely out of rooftop antenna range of any television stations (Baldwin & McVoy, 1988, p.5).

In Brazil, the CATV systems were known as Dis-TV or Distribution Television and also preceded real cable services. It was only in October of 1969 that the modern cable communications were implemented in the U.S., as a result of the FCC requirement that CATV systems with 3,500 or more subscribers start to originate programming (Jaffe, 1974). At this point, cable became a complementary service, usually in rural or distant communities served by less than three commercial stations. Even though Foster distinguishes cable TV from CATV by the offering of five different services—local stations, distant/imported signals, origination, pay and access (FCC prescribed) channels—the main benefit of cable was the clear reception of a television channel barely available over the air (Foster, 1982). The concept of cable as a multichannel programming source and, therefore, as a competitor to the networks, was developed in the 1970s through many lobbying and marketing victories. On legal grounds, the government policies that limited cable growth were gradually reversed.

First, operators had to convince the FCC that they could import signals from distant stations without harming the businesses of independent local UHF stations. Then, they had to conquer the right to coexist with Over-the-air television in the larger cities as well. By 1973, the FCC freeze on cable construction in the nation's 100 largest cities had been lifted, and in 1980 the importation of distant signals was allowed, attracting new investors. Considered "the way of the future," cable even attracted investments from the networks. The parent companies of the three nets were pressured by the stock market to enter cable. If they didn't, they would be considered "behind the times" and their stock would be undervalued (1983a). The conquest of city markets, though, proved not as easy as the traditional rural areas cable had dominated. Although building costs rise faster than population densities in rural areas, a study by cable consultant Paul Kagan concluded in 1972 that, as a rule, a rural cable system that enrolled 30 percent of homes passed could pay its own way. In the cities, where the cable plant costs are higher and there usually are more stations providing better signal reception, cable needed a stronger sales pitch. A report of the Sloan Commission on Cable Communications in 1972 estimated that only 15 percent of potential subscribers in large cities could be persuaded to subscribe to improve reception, the main benefit sought by rural subscribers (MacGregor, 1973). The marketing victory came with the introduction of cable-exclusive channels, delivered nationally by satellite, transforming cable into an alternative source of television. Videoclips, news, cartoons, documentaries, movies and other genres that shared fragments of the broadcasting hours became 24-hour lineups.

In 1972, the pay-per-channel idea was inaugurated by Home Box Office (HBO), a Time-Life (now Time-Warner) channel distributed by the group's cable operator in New York, the Manhattan Cable (Hoineff, 1991). The huge investments necessary were partly financed by large cable operators, the so-called multiple system operators (MSOs), conscious of the value of original programming. A 1988 Frank N. Magid Associates survey indicated that 82 percent of cable subscribers in the United States thought the enhanced image was the main reason for subscribing, while 93 percent said better and more varied programming was the main reason (Hoineff, 1991). Some of these new channels, like MTV, CNN, TNT and ESPN, were arriving in Brazil by the mid 90s through exclusive contracts with over-the-air systems, which had also retransmitted the signals to some of the incipient cable systems in the country. For American programmers, overseas cable offered another outlet for films and an opportunity to amortize production costs over an even broader base (1983b). In fact, the ever increasing production budgets and the multiplication of competitor channels had been some of the major problems of the whole American television industry in the 1980s, making other markets, like the Brazilian one, an attractive alternative.

The multiplication of programmers supported by Hollywood studios could finally bring the diversity the FCC had always called for, but the American audience was watching much less television than it was offered. The competition for the fragmenting audience reached a point that led some cable channels to pay cable operators for carrying and, without an audience rate system, the growth of advertising revenue was slow. The interest existed, though. In 1981, when penetration was 28 percent, advertisers were reviving trends from the early days in the production of programs and infomercials (3-10 minute messages). An article in Business Week magazine comments:

> Besides the extra control over the programming, advertisers faced cheaper production costs, which are about $2.5 million for a network two-hour show. A half hour of client supported programming usually cost $3 to 15 thousand. Others were not producing, but sponsoring programs, enjoying the possibility of having commercials of non-standard duration ... (1981b).

Most cable networks, however, made the mistake of believing that cable could be supported by advertising, just like broadcasting. In 1983 only seven cable channels reached 15 percent of all U. S. homes to be rated by Nielsen, and advertisers were actually scared of cable. The market demand for original programming was also reaching a borderline and new channels were having more difficulties in insuring successful launches. It took five years for Showtime to reach 2.8 million subscribers and finally break-even in 1982, the same period HBO took to break-even in 1977 with only 750,000 subscribers (1982a). In a turnaround, television entrepreneur Ted Turner charged operators a per-subscriber fee for carrying his channels—the superstation TBS (an independent UHF station retransmitted via satellite), the controversial all-news CNN and TNT's MGM library. He knew that advertising would not be enough in the short term and had an average 50 percent of revenues coming from operators. Others, like MTV, followed his idea and the timing for this change in sales strategy was right. According to the National Cable Television Association (NCTA), about 400,000 new subscribers were added per month in the early 1980s, while there was a merger fever that reduced the offer of programming, leaving operators in a bad position and very willing to pay (1983a).

Cable advertising revenues remained scarce. In 1990, they totaled $1, 393 million or just 1.1 percent of the total advertising volume in America (Monush, 1992). The almost exclusive dependence on subscriber fees caused significant price increases and government threats to reregulate the industry. Since the probable target of a new regulation would be to ensure the availability of locally originated channels at "reasonable" prices, many cable operators also redefined their service tiering to restrict the so-called basic service to these future regulated channels. The most common tierings in the 1990s defined basic service as the local channels, the public broadcasting and local access channels; enhanced services included most of the cable networks and premium service was comprised of pay-channels (HBO, Cinemax, Showtime, etc.) (Annis, 1992).

Moreover, operators were preparing themselves for a bloody competition with local telephone companies, which had been allowed in 1992 to enter the cable business. Counting on an infrastructure many times larger than the cable operators', the regional Bell telephone companies (RBOCs) were proposing to combine several services— like TV, telephone and computer communications—through a single cable connection. Cable operators, on the other hand, were striking back with the promise to change coaxial cables to fiber optics that allow up to 154 channels (Hoineff, 1991) of communication. Installed by MSOs or RBOCs, the systems of the future were generally expected to become broadband integrated digital services networks (ISDN) that, within the television scope, would offer two-way communication programs and several pay-per-view channels.

The Brazilian cable industry was believed to be much farther from this brilliant future, but those who did not believe in the possibilities of cable in Brazil had to only check what was going on at the Telebras research center in Campinas, São Paulo, where plans to implement pilot ISDN plants in the country were well advanced by the late 80s (Graciosa, 1988). And, in cities with a confusing underground network of cables, as was the case in most Brazilian cities, the thinner fiber optics was seen as the only solution for the installation of cable systems (Hoineff, 1991). In fact, most of the delay in the Brazilian cable development could be attributed to legislative problems. Many cable entrepreneurs believed that the emphasis on the economic obstacles may be over dimensioned in many cable-related studies. Brazil was one of the last countries in Latin America to institutionalize cable, ten years after Argentina and much after Chile, Colombia or Bolivia (Hoineff, 1991). The updated law on the industry still awaited definition in the early 90s, and the few entrepreneurs who had started construction by then were betting high. In January 1991, the estimated cost to build a cable system was $100,000, and a cable subscription was $400 (Schwartsman, 1991a).

4.3.1 Cable's legal battles in Brazil

The attempts to implement cable television in Brazil date back as far as the 1970s. In 1971, Globo network, already an American-like well-structured television system, developed a strong interest in the new technology and created the TVC company. Electronic engineer Wilson Brito worked for Globo at that time and was invited to participate in the enterprise. A short time after, he became the sole owner of TVC, as the network inexplicably lost interest on the project (1979b) .The few existing plants two decades later lead one to think that Globo acted wisely, forecasting a scenario where politics would delay appropriate legislation, and initiatives—even from the government—would be torn apart. That was the case in 1974, when the Communication Ministry denied authorization for the Federal University of Rio Grande do Sul to implement an experimental cable service in a small nearby community (1979b).

But if the government was not fostering the growth of cable television , it was certainly not unaware of it. For eight years, several research studies with unknown results had been conducted for the military governments. One of these studies was performed by Cesar Valente and Luis Lanzetta, professors at Federal University of Santa Catarina, and by journalist Daniel Herz. In an interview published later, they reported that the Communications Ministry and some group of entrepreneurs were defending the immediate implementation of cable services. Universities and researchers, on the other hand, preferred a cautious implementation, conditioned to "deep studies" and the elaboration of a complex and democratic legislation. And they revealed that these later groups were leading a movement for the de-acceleration of the implementation of cable services in Brazil (1979b). Under such circumstances, and still suffering the negative public relations effects of the recent denial of a license to Rio Grande do Sul University, the National Secretary of Telecommunications, Rômulo Furtado, rushed to present a decree in 1975 to regulate cable services in Brazil. The president at that time, Garrastazú Medici, never ratified the decree, but Furtado, who survived three other presidents in the government, tried again in 1979. This time, his proposal included some of the previous demands by the intellectual groups, like strict rules for the qualification of franchisees, mostly foundations and universities.

Nevertheless, he defended that cable technology was similar to radio-diffusion and did not require further studies by Brazilian universities before being regulated. The debates were switched to the social value of cable and the authority of regulation itself. Many politicians in charge of the communications policies were against the implementation of cable TV, because it was considered an elitist service promoted by foreign interests for an underdeveloped country, having no social value. In this manner, the strong opposition by nationalist general Andrade Serpa is said to have had the most negative impact on Furtado's proposal (1991d). Overwhelmed by a demand for 15 telephones per hundred habitants—while there were only six—the government had to agree that cable TV did not justify investments from the State, as it attended to a restricted group. Nevertheless, Furtado tried to indicate that the growth of the cable industry had positive effects, like the amplification of the job market and the preservation of regional cultures through increasing the viability of more local program productions. As the manufacturers of cable and wire for telecommunication in Brazil were mostly multinational companies, cable services were pointed to as the exclusive interest of foreign

101

groups and, therefore, against the "national sovereignty."

Furtado's challenge was to prove his point that cable technology was controlled by national companies, with 83 percent of the investment spent within the country in the national currency. The opposition was also concerned that the regulation should be implemented through a law voted by Congress and not an Executive decree, as proposed. However, the Brazilian Telecommunication Code, law number 4.117 voted by the National Congress in 1962—when not even the videotape existed—attributed to the Executive power, the authority to create special telecommunication services through decree (1979a). In spite of all the opposition, by late 1982 the proposal was under final revision. A broad perspective was adopted, with services like computer connections and bidirectional communication planned through the use of fiber optics. The project stated that franchisees named by the Ministry of Communications would have to carry, besides their own programming, all channels freely offered in their operation area. The service was to be paid by subscribers and the fees charged would be defined by the market. Telephone ducts and poles could be used for the installation of cables. The channels would be operated through a rental contract and would have to be yielded to public service operations whenever necessary (1982b). But it was not until 1988 that Brazil got its first legislation for cable television. Decree 143 signed by the Communications Ministry on June 21, 1988 authorized the simple reception of signals through a collective antenna and their redistribution by cable (Duó, 1989b). Restrictive and bureaucratic, it was not a legal piece to foster the industry growth, but it definitely was an important first step.

Operating like a Community Antenna Television (CATV), these systems required three authorizations to be established: from the networks whose images would be distributed; from Embratel, the state satellite company, allowing it to receive signals via satellite; and from the National Telecommunication Department (Dentel), indicating the area attended to by the service. Pioneer plants, like the one in Presidente Prudente (580 kilometers west of São Paulo city), complained several times that their requests for redistribution authorization were never answered by the networks, while Dentel was surprisingly quick in shutting them down. Unlike American cable legislation, the generation of images and the distribution of signals from Intelsat were prohibited, but no mention was made of charges for the distribution service (Duó, 1989a). Apart from these real problems, many entrepreneurs started developing plants and, for 1989, many headlines previewed a boom in cable plants, expecting up to 300 new systems in the country as a whole (Duó, 1989b). The euphoria in that year was so great that 36 entrepreneurs in the cable TV area created the Associação Brasileira das Antenas Comunitárias (Abracom) or, in English, Brazilian Association of Community Antennas, on July 28, to foster the new industry (Duó, 1989b). Some of these first experiences happened in Presidente Prudente area, Goiânia (capital of Goiás state), and even in a condominium at the suburbs of São Paulo city. Although it only retransmitted the national channels, Presidente Prudente is acknowledged as the first city in Brazil to have a cable system, starting right after the legislation was implemented, in the middle of 1988.

On June 6, 1988, the 16,000 inhabitants of the city of Santo Anastácio—a few miles from Presidente Prudente—became the second. The person responsible for this latter experience was father José Antonio de Lima, who installed two parabolic antennas next to the church and a small studio in his house. Before that, the city could watch only two channels. A month later, the 250 customers already listed had a potential for 35 channels. Initially, they could watch all national networks and five foreign channels: Spain 1 and 2, NBC, Bright Star and C-Span (Duó, 1989b). A local channel transmitted two movies a day, paying only NCz$10 (ten cruzados novos[6]) a month, which was reinvested in the maintenance of the plant and the payment of three employees, the service was not restricted to an elite. The investment of $41,000 was financed by TV Cabo do Brasil also responsible for the plant in Presidente Prudente, and by Huler, the Argentine electronic industry. Installing their own poles, and even using the light towers of some houses, the entrepreneurs decided to transform Santo Anastácio into a laboratory for other projects, which TV Cabo was franchising

6   The currency in Brazil has changed from cruzeiros (Cr$) to cruzados (Cz$), then cruzados novos (NCz$) and back to cruzeiros in the 90s before settling on reais. In most cases, the changes were accompanied by economic reforms and cuts in the number of zeros in each bill. See chart in appendix for dollar equivalent.

in other parts of the country (Duó, 1989b). TV Cabo of Goânia sprang out of these experiences. The $600,000 invested there was expected to start paying a financial return within four years. In April 1991 the system already had 1,000 subscribers, attending to an area of 900 blocks in the richest neighborhood of the city. The subscriber paid Cr$60,000 for the installation and the decoder, and Cr$4,000 as a monthly fee (França, 1991).

Exempt from the restrictions on generating images, closed communities, like rich condominiums, also started developing cable systems, usually bringing television signals to hard-to-reach areas. Barra da Tijuca in Rio was soon a prospect market for cable. It had problems receiving the television signals due to its mountainous location, and the acquisitive power of its residents was high enough to pay the estimated $150,000 investment (1979b). The Tamboré condominium plant, 30 kilometers from São Paulo city limits, is another initiative from that time. Approximately 700 houses were served with 40 channels, including a closed circuit that let the residents see on their TV sets the image of visitors in the entrance of the condominium. The $500,000 plant at the Tamboré condominium was the second built by Panavisão company, which had previously experimented with service to the 600 houses of the country club Pro-Vida, in Sorocaba (92 kilometers east of São Paulo city), with a micro system built in 1986. The prospects of financial return within two years, according to company executives, really explain why these plants became an attractive business in Brazil (Duó, 1989c). But, following the American definition previously presented, those cannot be considered real cable systems, which are allowed to insert advertising into the programming and even to generate their own images. Such a distinction came with another decree, number 250, signed in December 1989 at the end of the Sarney government by the Ministry of Communications, Antonio Carlos Magalhães. The so-called Service of Television Signals Distribution (DISTV) (1991d) had a very simple application process, as well as political importance. The National Communications Secretary simply acknowledged—or not—the right of a company to provide the DisTV service as it intended to do. For the real cable TV service (with ads and generation of programs), the Secretary planned a more complex legislation (Carla, 1991).

It was 1991 and approximately 5,000 people were already watching cable TV in Brasil (Arruda, 1991). But on March 20, the applications for DisTV were suspended until new rules could be implemented. A proposal for cable service regulation was published on June 10 in the Diário Oficial da União and there were many changes to the prior legislation. The 18-page decree was written by communications engineer Sávio Pinheiro, with several elements of the American legislation. The prospective franchisees, for example, were required to file application informing the region of service, the area attended to and the number of channels provided, besides a viability study, programming definition, installation chronogram and number of households attended to within two years. Having received the application, the SNC would publish a note in the Official Daily giving a waiting period during which other companies could dispute the application. Each franchise would be valid for ten years and was limited to Brazilian companies with national capital (at least 51 percent of share capital owned by native Brazilians) (Bensimon, 1991).

To avoid monopolistic practices, the decree established that whoever already had communications companies—radio, newspaper or conventional TV—in the same city would lose points in the application evaluation. The maximum number of franchises in one city was 20, and multiple ownership was conditioned to the size of the cities (a maximum of four systems in cities with more than one million inhabitants, ten systems in cities between 300,000 and one million inhabitants, and 30 systems in cities with less than 300,000 inhabitants) (1991s). The offer of local and educational programs was mandatory, and the renewal of the franchise was conditioned to a positive plebiscite by the subscribers. Abusive increases in the fees, or contract violations, were punished accordingly, with fee, suspension of services for a determined period or termination of franchise (1991h). The proposal fixed July 2, 1991 as the date for a public audience about the subject, and many entrepreneurs and social groups were present to defend their interests.

Again, the general complaint, embodied by the National Forum for the Democratization of Communication Media, was the implementation of law through an Executive decree, instead of Congressional vote. They indicated the recent 1988 Constitution, in its chapter V, where it stated that the distribution of television channels must follow criteria of social interest. The government, however, classified cable TV as a special service of a private nature, that is, only the paying subscribers can watch it. The Brazilian Communication Code of 1962 guaranteed the president's exclusive powers to distribute such concessions. When the franchises were suspended in 1991, 95 had already been distributed (40 by Collor and the rest by Sarney), and the various companies were anxious to have legislation that would allow them to start profiting. Many of them were afraid that, if the proposal had to be approved by Congress, no law would ever be implemented, due to a strong negative lobby from over-the-air subscription stations (Arruda, 1991). The strong political character of these concessions indicated that their fear was substantiated. About half of the 95 franchisees did not intend to meet the demands of the decree. In spite of the application fee, equal to four percent of the project value, a large number of companies were ghost ones, without any address, and most applicants did not have any qualifications. Istoé/Senhor magazine published the story of Bayard Umbuzeiro, owner of a transporting company, city deputy in Santos (a São Paulo state port), and close friend of the Infrastructure Minister, who—in spite of his inexperience in the sector—took only 21 days to create seven projects for cable plants. When all of the projects were approved, Umbuzeiro was to face the need for an investment of approximately $1 million for each plant, going up to $8 million if the equipment used was from the last generation (1991x).

But there were also real entrepreneurs in the business. In Capão Novo, a beach condominium in the north of Rio Grande do Sul, Pan Sat, a parabolic antenna manufacturer, invested $3.5 million in 1990 to build a sophisticated cable plant. Part of the 60,000 meters of cable line were financed by 1,200 subscriptions, from a calculated total of more than 250,000, and with a potential to grow by 200 outlets a year. Authorized by the government to provide cable services, Pan Sat signed technology transfer contracts with four Canadian companies: Conrad, Beckerman, Nexus and Norsat. Canadian technicians also coordinated a group of 40 Brazilians in the implementation of the system, which fixed cables to the local electric company's poles. Equipment like cables, satellite receivers, modulators, cameras and videotext had to be imported. The company was set to run the system in Capão Novo for ten years; the official starting date was January 5,

1991. The 17 channels initially defined were to be captured by parabolic antennas from Brasilsat and PanamSat. The local channels were to be received through a special link from the nearby retransmission stations. The foreign channels were to be CNN, ESPN, RAT, Mexico TV and National TV of Chile. Locally generated programs were also scheduled, providing information about the condominium's internal activities. For this service, each subscriber paid an inauguration fee in January 1991, which totaled approximately Cr$66,900, besides a monthly maintenance fee (Arruda, 1990).

Surrounded by mountains, the television reception at Alphaville, a rich condominium 27 kilometers from São Paulo, was never good until the beginning of 1991. That was when resident Guilherme Stoliar, executive vice-president of SBT (Sistema Brasileiro de Televisão), the second-largest broadcast network in the country, decided to implement a cable system in the neighborhood. With Marcos Amazonas, who was also involved in the first days of MTV Abril, they decided to make the area a "show-room" for their new cable company. The 22,400 meters of cable were to initially service 700 houses of the 5,000 built in the condominium, which also had 9,000 empty lots (1991a). For $580, divided into six monthly installments, and a monthly fee of $40, the subscriber received 25 channels, with potential to expand up to 60. The pay channels of GloboSat or TVA, which associated itself to the TV Alphaville system, were elected by the residents. The five parabolic antennas, three editing tables and a little studio were designed to offer a very sophisticated array of services. Besides a closed circuit channel that allowed condominium visitors to be seen on TV sets, the locally produced programming was to offer English classes, recipes, computer-accessed databases, and traffic and weather information through an interactive system. The $1.5 million investment had a break-even point of 1,000 subscribers, with each one paying $1,100 (1991a). Ribeirão Preto and Franca, two cities of São Paulo, also received authorization to build cable plants. Franca received a green light in 1989 and started operations only in 1991, due to difficulties with the local electric company over the use of poles. After building their own poles, they started a subscription campaign that conquered 1,400 subscribers in two months, paying an yearly fee of Cr$45,000 (1991u).

Video producer Sérgio Adaid of TV Video a Cabo Belo Horizonte Ltda. inaugurated a cable plant in a neighborhood of Belo Horizonte, the capital of Minas Gerais state, on April 5, 1991. Created four months before, the company already listed 540 subscribers by its inauguration. The company expected to add 40, 000 viewers in three years by expanding the service to the other 24 neighborhoods of the city. With the capacity to carry up to 35 channels, the system started operating with 12 channels: the six national networks and six foreign channels. The plans were to have CNN, ESPN, TVT (24-hour subtitled movies), C-Span, the Spanish TVE International and Italian RAI (two hours a day). The $290,000 investment included the purchase of the whole physical plant from Argentine Novatek, responsible for more than 40 other cable plants in Latin America. The initial price per subscription was Cr$130,000 and the monthly fee was Cr$3,800 (Nicolau, 1991). In the South, the powerful independently owned Group RBS, affiliated to Globo network, won 17 of the 43 concessions distributed in Rio Grande do Sul and Santa Catarina.

A campaign of $80,000 launched VTV - Televisão a Cabo Ltda. of Curitiba, capital of Paraná in April of 1991. Attending to 15,000 subscribers initially, the company owned by the well known journalists Ivan Carta and Bernardo Rosemann had already invested $1 million in the project. The initial package offered to 24,000 households in three neighborhoods included foreign channels RAI (Italian), CNN, TNT, and ESPN(USA), Prime (English), TV Chile, Argentina TV Color, TVE (Spain), Televisa (Mexico) and Televen (Venezuela). Such programming cost $2 per month per subscriber. With technology by the Canadian company Lindsay, the system had 50,000 meters of cables installed on electric company poles. A previous survey indicated that about 75 percent of the residents (of the three neighborhoods) were interested in having the system, which had a monthly price of Cr$6,000 (Monteiro, 1991a). The cable legislation proposal under study by the government was expected to be implemented by September 1991. It was not implemented by the time of this study, but in any case it did not mention the current concession holders. The government could recognize the rights of present franchisees—with systems built or not—or it could redistribute the concessions so as to leave politically uninteresting groups out of a game potentially worth $60 million within four years (1991x). In the aftermath of President

Collor impeachment in the early 90s, any forecast on such a matter was impossible at the time of the study.

4.4 Satellites: a future reflected in the skies

In 1992, the Brazilian satellite program celebrated its first decade. It was on June 7, 1982 that the military government signed the contract with Arianespace to launch the BrasilSat, built by the Spar consortium. The total cost of $210 million was considered exorbitant in face of the overall poverty of the country, but the program has certainly achieved its purpose (1982d). Scholars like Omar Souki de Oliveira define the military goals in the following terms:

> The generals believed in the geopolitical advantages of unifying the land and the people, who should speak one language (Portuguese) and hold allegiance to one nation (Brazil). To that effect they used television via satellite. The telecommunications sector received particular attention, substituting the old terrestrial microwave links with two stationary satellites. Today 99 percent of Brazilian territory is covered by the medium (Oliveira, 1992).

On February 8, 1985, BrasilSat AI was launched, followed by BrasilSat AII on March 28, 1986 (Arrudão, 1990). The ground segment, though, started to be setup much earlier to make use of the first international satellite services, created in the 1960s. Brazil was one of the 50 countries that originally composed the International Telecommunications Satellite consortium (Intelsat) in August 1965, with one percent of the shares the equivalent annual volume of its system utilization. The Empresa Brasileira de Telecomunicações (Embratel), created in September 1964 to operate the satellite communications, rushed to build an Earth station at Itaboraí, Rio de Janeiro. Tanguá was inaugurated on February 28, 1969 with a 30-meter parabolic antenna to send and receive signals through 268 voice channels and two television channels (Sampaio, 1984). In 1976, Brazil increased its shares to 4.36 percent, becoming the fourth largest shareholder among 100 country members, after the USA (26.7 percent), United Kingdom (11.14 percent) and France (5.8 percent) (Vampré, 1979). In the beginning of the 1990s, the Intelsat system totaled about 120 countries operating 15 geosynchronous satellites over Atlantic, Pacific and Indian Ocean and more than 800 ground stations. This network serves around 170 countries and territories, being responsible for two-thirds of all intercontinental telephone calls, besides the majority of television transmissions (Hoineff, 1991). Thus, even though the Americans developed the communication satellite system, Brazil can be considered an early and relatively heavy user of it, jumping on the bandwagon as soon as the medium proved useful.

From the initial conceptualization by writer Arthur C. Clarke to the launch of Early Bird, the first commercial communications satellite, the Americans overcame many drawbacks to build the medium, which is now internationalized (See Table 9). In the 1990s, however, the U.S. government had opposed this internationally controlled satellite system, stating that:

> Intelsat's monopoly is inefficient, its rates do not reflect actual costs, and its sheer size makes it inflexible. Competition from smaller, nimbler satellite firms, they contend, would lower prices for all, enhance services, and encourage innovation (Head & Sterling, 1990, p.515).

This new policy reflected the growing interest of American companies for satellite services in the 1980s. By 1981, there were nine domestic satellites serving the United States with all 24 transponders of each one already occupied. Cable networks were major users, but some companies were just holding transponders against future use or for resale. A BusinessWeek article tells the story of cable consultant Timothy Flynn, who requested a Satcom transponder in 1979, paying $250,000 for its rights, and sold his leasing privilege to Warner Communications two years later for $5.5 million. Flynn was benefiting from FCC legislation that considered space satellite companies as common carriers that should provide space on a first-come, first-served basis for monthly fees between $50,000 and $150,000 and limited profits. In 1981, Hughes Communications International, which was planning to launch the $100 million Galaxy I, defied the FCC rules by selling its transponders instead of leasing them. With sales to Time, Westinghouse, Times Mirror and Turner Broadcasting for prices between $8 and $10 million, Hughes proved that there was a demand for satellite services that common carriers could not appropriately explore (1981a).

Table 9 - Satellite developments

Initial American Experiences		
Passive Reflectors		
ECHO I, II	1960	First to carry transponders orbited the Earth in 90 minutes, remaining in line of sight for approximately 15 minutes
Medium Height Active Reflectors		
TELSTAR	1962	In this year, U.S. Congress enacted the RELAY Communication Satellite ct. Private company COMSAT authorized to launch and operate a world satellite system
High Active Synchronous Repetitor		
SYNCOM I, II	1964	First with synchronous orbit about 2,300 miles above the equator
International Consortium		
Intelsat I	1965	(Early Bird) 50 MHz bandwidth
Intelsat II	1967	130 MHz bandwidth
Intelsat III	1968	300 MHz bandwidth
Intelsat IV	1971	500 MHz bandwidth
Intelsat IV-A	1975	800 MHz bandwidth
Intelsat V	1980	2,144 MHz bandwidth
Intelsat V-A	1985	2,250 MHz bandwidth
Intelsat VI	1989	3,300 MHz bandwidth

Source: Head, Sydney W. and Sterling, Christopher H. Broadcasting in America: A Survey of Electronic Media. 6th Edition. Boston, Houghton Mifflin Co., 1990

By the mid 90s, the equator was congested with about 150 satellites in geosynchronous orbit, but this number was expected to reach up to 200 satellites by the end of the century. The increased offer reduced costs. It was estimated that between 1975 and 1985 the real cost for renting space in an American domestic satellite dropped more than 120 percent (Hoineff, 1991). In 1986 the FCC authorized several satellite companies to launch separate systems, bypassing

Intelsat in the Atlantic. Many member nations protested, foreseeing a loss of the most profitable services that may even force a change in Intelsat's cross-subsidy policy, favoring smaller countries with lighter communication traffic. The national telecommunication companies, which usually enjoy a monopoly on the lucrative terrestrial segments (all satellite connections tend to be funneled to their few Earth stations) also opposed the bypass. Private satellite operators could then establish direct links to consumers who erect their own Earth stations or even buy smaller parabolic antennas. Pan American Satellite Corporation (PAS) was the first such American private company to launch a satellite to provide services to the United States, Central and South America, the Caribbean and Europe. The PanamSat was launched on September 1988 by the Alpha Lyracom group, and 18 of its 24 transponders were focused on Peru and Brazil. In spite of the American cable networks' interest in relaying their programs to Latin America, few companies or government agencies were eager to face the heavy investments or legal obstacles to settle contracts. Gradually, Peru, Dominican Republic and Costa Rica signed up, joined by Britain, Ireland, Luxembourg, Sweden and Germany on the other side of the Atlantic (Head & Sterling, 1990). PanamSat was planned to have ten to 13 years of life and its operators would invest $310 million in that period, including construction and launch (1989b).

The new American satellite services caught Brazil in a very different scenario from the early days of the Brazilian satellite program. The military regime was over and, with it, its huge investments in telecommunications. Some denunciations indicated that "at the end of 1987, official data (most likely inflated) counted 20 of the 24 transponders at one BrasilSat satellite in use, but none in the other" (Oliveira, 1992). In fact, Embratel controlled 24 transponders, but only 22 were operational, while two were kept in reserve in case any of the others failed. Two kinds of BrasilSat services were offered for transmission of television signals via satellite: TVSat, for television networks, and TV Executiva, a closed circuit for the use of banks and other companies. Some networks leased full and others half transponders. The TV networks that demand full permanent transponders were Globo, Bandeirantes, Manchete, SBT, TVE/ Funteve (Rio de Janeiro) and Jovem Pan. They paid Cr$40 million, and each additional programmed 30-minute use cost Cr$92, 000. Half permanent transponders were used by Abril/MTV, Record, TV Rio and TV Brasil Oeste. They paid Cr$24.42 million and each additional programmed 30-minute use costs Cr$56,000. Regional TVSats operated with two half transponders shared among various regional TV networks and, in this case, the rent of permanent services cost from Cr$10 to $18 million. Embratel operated closed-circuit services only with half transponders, in a total of 12. GloboSat had four, TVA had three, TV Gaúcha had one and KTV Comunicações Ltda. had two. Two of these half transponders were shared by several companies. Each half transponder cost Cr$45 million per month (Magalhães, 1991).

Both services—TVSat and TV Executiva—could be utilized in a permanent (all the time) or programmed (only specific moments) manner. But, with the exception of the networks, these transponders had usually been used for short periods. A satellite rush, as happened in America, came only five years after the launching of BrasilSat II. In April 1991, GloboSat (under the legal name of Horizonte Comunicações leased four transponders, followed in July by TVA (Rádio Enlace Ltda.) with three more and, in August, TV Gaúcha (RBS Group) leased the last one available. The two pay-TV companies (GloboSat and TVA) not only assured their operations with the transponders, but also precluded possible competitors from entering the business until 1994, when a new Brazilian satellite was scheduled to be launched. BrasilSat B1 and B2 were scheduled for 1994 and 1996, respectively) (Apolinário, 1991). The addition of PanamSat services complemented the larger use of national satellites in the increase of this system's value. It was through the PanamSat that American cable programming became available in Brazil. Test transmissions via PanamSat started on November 8, 1988, and the U.S. version of CNN started to be freely delivered in December.

Two years later, the recently created CNN International replaced it with scrambled signals reaching houses and commercial stations in the country thanks to a breach in the national legislation. Embratel had a monopoly on commercial telecommunications in the country and, by contract, it could only distribute signals received from Intelsat. The reception of signals by private parabolic antennas was not legally restricted or controlled, however (Hoineff, 1991). In

1988, the 120,000 backyard dish owners in Brazil, who were used to a traditional limitation to the AERTS (Armed Forces Radio and Television Services) programming, welcomed the new satellite services. Freely capturing signals from three international satellites and two domestic ones, their programming options were more varied than ever (See Table 10). Even though technically unauthorized, the reception of satellite-relayed television signals not intended for public viewing was tolerated for a long time. While the American cable networks had nothing to lose, since there was no pay television system in Brazil, the national networks increased their audiences, even though the commercials were not seen (due to the local character of most advertising, they are not carried by the satellite) (Hoineff, 1991). The parabolic dish antenna manufacturers, too, were enthusiastic. Biasia Company, for example, experienced a nine-month growth of 150 percent, conquering 20 percent of the market with the production of 2,000 antennas and 2,500 receivers in the beginning of 1992.

The Brazilian parabolic antenna market was disputed by six large companies that, together, produced around 18,000 antennas per month, while in the United States this number was 50,000 per month (Moreira, 1992). The free tuning bonanza did not last, though. The launch of GloboSat in 1991 was coincident with the codification of Globo TV images, transmitted through BrasilSat II, and the scrambling of CNN and TNT signals on the PanamSat satellite. Other South beam channels followed suit, as American channels did in the U.S. after 1986, when Home Box Office (HBO) scrambled its pay-TV service. Curiously, it was also HBO that, in 1975, inaugurated the satellite-cable relationship, transmitting its signal through Satcom I to cable operators all over the United States (Hoineff, 1991). The move in the United States was intended to protect cable subscribers, who were paying for what the programming dish owners were getting free, as they bypassed the cable operators. The fact was that most dish owners were not served by any cable company and were not able to receive any television over the air either. As more and more channels were scrambled, a very small percentage of the dish owners in America became subscribers (See Table 11). The average fees of around $150 per year were considered too high and the majority of dish owners was only concerned about the possibility of the three broadcast networks scrambling (1987). Even though São Paulo was estimated as having

Table 10 - What is seen through a parabolic antenna in Brazil

Signals captured from Gorizont, Intelsat, PanamSat and BrasilSat II:	
● Russian TV	news, events and sports
● French TV	variety
● TVE/ Spain	
● Cadena Audio Esporádio Colombia	
● Televen/ Venezuela	
● Brighstar/ London-UK	
● NBC/ London-UK	
● Worldnet/ USA	USIS, PBS and C-Span news
● TV Chile	
● TV Mexico	
● Telefe/Argentina	Half transponder, requires special antenna
● Japanese TV	Sunday programming, 1:30 to 3 PM
● Commercial TV/ Peru	
● ATC/ Argentina	
● CNN/ USA	Encoded
● TNT/ America	Encoded
● RAI International/ Italy	7 to 9 PM, encoded
● Globo/RJ	
● SBT/SP	
● TVE/RJ	
● Manchete/RJ	
● Bandeirantes/SP	
● Globo/ Manaus	Half transponder
● TV Abril-MTV/ SP	Half transponder
● TV Embratel	
● TV Rio	Half transponder
● Jovem Pan	

Source: (Boarini, 1991)

fewer than 15,000 parabolic antennas, the scrambling was depriving many people of their sole source of television. As was the case in the U.S., the majority of Brazilian dishes was located in places where

Table 11 - How American dish owners cope with scrambling

The survey results are based on the responses to four questionnaires that were bound into the April, May, June and July issues of Satellite Orbit magazine. More than 20,000 responses were received and tabulated. The figures reported reflect the percentage of readers who answered each question.

Have you bought or leased a VideoCipher II (descrambler)?

Yes	17%
No	83%

Does the local cable company sell satellite programming subscriptions to dish owners?

Yes	22%
No	78%

Do you feel your satellite TV system has been a worthwhile investment?

Yes	73%
No	27%

When you bought your satellite TV system, were you aware that some services would be scrambled and available by subscriptions only?

Yes	44%
No	56%

What is the total amount you pay per month for programming subscriptions?

Less than $15	37%
$15 to $30	36%
$30 to $45	19%
$45 to $60	4%
More than $60	4%

What type of area do you live in?

Rural	72%
Suburban	20%
Urban	8%

Do you have access to cable TV?

Yes	22%
No	78%

Source: Satellite Orbit magazine, September 1987, p.20-7

television was not at hand: the rural areas and, especially, the Northeast region of Brazil, where large farms and sparse communities prevail (Delmanto, 1991).

4.4.1 From TVRO to SMATV and DBS

The military regime's satellite program was not limited to the federal level in Brazil. Since the 1960s, the mayors of many small cities bought TVROs (television receive-only antennas) to bring one or more channels to town. The local advertising spots available proved to be useful not only to the businesses in the area, but for political purposes as well. The smaller cities invested in relatively inexpensive TVROs that were six to eight meters in diameter, just large enough to compensate for the low power (less than 100 watts) of the traditional C-Band satellite-relayed signals, which were then rebroadcast locally through modest amplifiers/transmitters. The satellite relay of the new channels MTV and Jovem Pan, however, encountered reception problems in many of these cities. Engineer Lucrécia Costa, from Jovem Pan, explained that the old dish-receiver equipment was not always adequate, and better receivers were necessary to receive the weaker signals delivered by channels using half transponders.

In the United States, the TVROs multiplied after 1979, when the FCC eliminated a problematic and expensive licensing process. Cable and broadcast stations quickly shifted from land to satellite relays and, as the technology improved to smaller and cheaper antennas, households out of the reach of standard television service became new clients. As Head and Sterling summarize:

> About two million backyard dishes, on the order of six to ten feet in diameter, had been installed in the United States by 1989. They can pick up as many as 150 different programs from domestic satellites, many of them private relays, such as news feeds, not intended for public consumption. These home pickups became known as C-band direct reception because C-band satellite users normally intend their transmissions for designated intermediate addressees, not for direct reception by the general public (Head & Sterling, 1990, p.173).

117

The success of C-band (3 to 6 GHz) satellite-delivered television revealed a potential market for the high-powered short-wave Ku-band (11 to 15 GHz) transponders, which allow the use of smaller antennas, between one and three feet in diameter. Thus, in June 1982, the FCC allocated 500 MHz (12.2 to 12. 7 GHz) to the new Direct Broadcast Satellites (DBS) designed to provide services specifically for home reception. After a few years, though, seven of the eight original applicants gave up, including Comsat's Satellite Telecommunications Corporation, which closed its doors in November 1984, after accumulating $140 million losses in five and a half years of operation (Yuster, 1992). Among the new round of eight applicants granted permits in 1988, Hughes Communications was the only one still promising to launch a DBS service by 1994[7]. In the meantime, cable operators have gotten together to explore a quasi-DBS service via conventional medium-power fixed satellites. This service can only use three- or four-foot dishes, but it was suspected to be just a move to preempt any high-power DBS enterprises (Yuster, 1992).

The launching campaign of GloboSat services in 1991 promoted it as the first DBS system in Brazil, leaving many people confused. Actually, GloboSat was more properly called a C-band direct-reception system. The weak signals delivered by BrasilSat II, which relayd GloboSat's channels, were focused on the equator, and the receiving dishes could be smaller, the closer they were to the equator. In Pará, in northern Brazil, the dishes could have a minimum two-meter diameter, while in São Paulo they ought to be at least three meters. The most widely used ones were actually 4.65 meters in diameter. Thus, the real Ku-band DBS and its smaller dishes had not reached the country yet. Rumors at the time suggested that the next Brazilian satellite would be launched in 1994 with some Ku-band transponders, but the technicians expected that at least three of such satellites would be necessary to cover the whole Brazilian territory. According to information presented in a contemporary book by Nelson Hoineff, of Manchete TV, prospective DBS users were not to wait long. A DBS earth station, with higher power was under construction in Morungaba, São Paulo. Joining some of the first DBS services to reach the Americas—RAI, BBC World Service and Japan Satellite

7 Hughes did launch that year, beginning the DIRECTV DBS service in the U.S. and later expanding to Latin America by 1997.

Television—Intelsat k-4 was scheduled for launch sometime in 1992 with eight transponders directed to Europe, and eight to America. Two of them would be reserved for DBS transmission.

While the promise of a more sophisticated satellite system remained just that, a promise, the low-powered DBS services of GloboSat were conquering subscribers. By 1992, the industry estimated that 160,000 dishes were installed in Brazilian backyards, including those TVROs that served more than one household (Moreira, 1992). In this case, the earth stations could be more appropriately called SMATVs (Satellite Master Antenna Television). The first SMATVs appeared around 1980 in both the United States and Brazil and, since they operate on private land, usually serving an apartment building or group of buildings, their proliferation occurred independently of legislation. Hotel Maksoud Plaza in São Paulo installed such a system, offering 25 channels—all the commercial, the paid and the satellite-received ones. Three other channels showed events that occur in the hotel (1992c). And some English language schools are pulling cable from their backyard dishes to TV sets installed in each class or across different building units. The signals captured by a SMATV parabolic antenna were distributed by cable to the several households, making these earth stations a sort of mini-cable plant. Even though American cable operators are strong enemies of SMATVs, in Brazil these systems could very well be the seen as embryos of future cable plants, since one operator may be tempted to cross its fence to serve more houses. With its multitude of names and users, the satellite systems certainly illustrated the signal distribution technology that would support the expansion of all other systems in Brazil. STV, MMDS and cable depend on satellite relays. In the era of marketing segmentation, all the little segments in each market are brought together to recompose a mass audience on the national and international level thanks to the satellites.

5
Programming Segmentation

The time for extra effort is clearly when the situation is in doubt. When neither side has a clear-cut superiority. Winning the battle for sales leadership in a single year will often clench the victory for decades to come (Ries & Trout, 1981, p.54).

The establishment of new television signal distribution technologies in Brazil enlarged the programming offer significantly. About 188 hours of daily broadcasting were added by the main pay-TV companies in the market alone—TVA and GloboSat (See Table 1). If the 16- to 24-hour schedules of the new open UHF channels Jovem Pan and MTV-Abril are included, along with the 14 foreign television signals captured by satellite dish owners, this number is dramatically multiplied. But while the increase in television time was accompanied in America by more program production, the same does not seem to be happening in Brazil. The American example shows that a large portion of the cable companies were led to invest in the creation of networks with differentiated programming to fulfill the new channels made available and make cable television more attractive to prospective subscribers. Comparatively, the number of new channels created in Brazil was much smaller than in the United States, but enough to present a critical mass in the demand of new television programs. Identifying the audience niches not previously satisfied, and considering the social-economic conditions of Brazil, most of the new channels opted, however, for predominantly imported lineups.

According to Browne, the Brazilian option is the common alternative of most nations. "[Since] imported programs almost always are much cheaper than those made by the domestic system, ... most of the worlds television systems import more programs than they produce [This fact explains] the increasing homogeneity of TV

121

Table 1 - Total broadcasting hours added by new channels

Company/Channel	Daily hours	Program Nationality
TVA	114	
Filmes	24	USA (99%), European (1%)
Notícias (CNN)	24	USA
Esportes (ESPN)	24	USA
Supercanal	18	USA (99%), Italian (1%)
Clássicos (TNT)	24	USA
Globosat	74	
Filmes (Telecine)	24	USA (99%), European (1%)
Notícias (GNT)	16	USA/Europe (99%), Brazil
Esportes (Top Sports)	16	USA & Europe (99%), Brazil
Shows (Multishow)	18	German, Japanese, French
PluralSat	12	German, French
Open channels		
MTV-Abril	24	USA (50%), Brazilian (50%)
Jovem Pan	16	Mainly foreign
Grand Total	240	

Source: Abril, GloboSat and Jovem Pan - January 1992

programming schedules" (Browne, 1989). All of the recent changes in the global traffic of television programming suggest, however, that importation does not have to be a fact of life. The new Brazilian televisions companies that survive their initial tribulations and conquer a piece of the market will be inserted, it seems, into a scenario where they will have the option to co-produce with international partners and even become exporters.

In their initial stage, nevertheless, these young companies are expected to find that it is inconvenient to maintain parallel investments such as program production. Since the return of the initial investments have not been accomplished yet, heavy investments in equipment and specialized labor represent an extra debt not recoverable in the short term. Imported programs, tested and amortized in their original markets, are clearly better options. Moreover, the focused character of the new channels means that no large segments of the market will be reached to justify the prompt investment. Such circumstances are common to all new television systems, and the recently created private European channels have resorted to importation as well. If the American cable networks did not follow this importation trend it was because they relied heavily on old productions, which had their costs already amortized by broadcasters' exhibition and were cheaply available in the syndication market. Barnouw recalls that:

> Cable systems produced little that was new; ... each was a supermarket of items made largely by others. Spokesmen for the networks—still dominant but increasingly edgy—were fond of pointing out that cable schedules, when not featuring old movies, were often filled up with old television series—network hand-me-downs ... Cable spokesmen, in response, expressed satisfaction that they were helping television "classics" find a new audience, and noted that many viewers apparently found them preferable to current network fare (Barnouw, 1990).

The incredible program production of the United States represents a rather unique case with some contextual differences from Brazilian television. Initially, it is necessary to recognize that the expansion of television time occurred in Brazil much later than it did in the United States. The market environments are different, and it is possible to point out many reasons for the American production increase, as well as the Brazilian drive to importation. The latter, for example, can now count on a very developed international television market that simply did not exist at the time that cable entrepreneurs were growing in America. Moreover, as Chapter 6 further analyzes, there seems to exist a very controversial cultural difference between the two audiences. Brazilians (or at least the elite) are apparently more open to other cultures and programming—especially the First World ones—whereas the American audience seems to feel more comfortable with the particular characteristics of nationally produced programs.

Without the same open appreciation of international programs, pioneer American television, unlike the Brazilian, had its demand fulfilled by a powerful cinema industry. Owner of most equipment patents and counting on a large, wealthy market, the American cinema studios have invented and dominated with "iron clash" the feature film production worldwide. A 1973-83 study by Tapio Varis about sources of programs for TV stations in 50 countries indicated that the United States exported more than twice as many programs as all other countries combined. Moreover, in the USA, where more than 150 companies were involved in the mid-60s in the production and exportation of TV programs, the nine companies that formed the Motion Picture Export Association of America accounted for about 80 percent of the total American sales abroad (Varis, 1974). Ultimately concentrated into a handful of large companies, this industry takes advantage of a privileged market position to dictate the international program commercialization norms. Restricting the distribution of some movies or conditioning the sale of blockbuster productions to the purchase of second-class movies (of low repercussion), the American giants have sometimes ruined competitive industries in the process.

When Brazilian television started to demand more programs, the unfair practices of American distributors in Brazil had already caused the decline of a once vigorous cinema industry. And since Brazilian broadcasters had to develop their own program production centers, there was no independent production industry to serve the new channels now. By operating both as producers and exhibitors, the Brazilian networks closed the doors to independent production for a long time. Globo, for example, produced up to 95 percent of its own primetime schedule. It was only in the 1980s that new technological improvements reduced the cost of TV equipment, allowing many small entrepreneurs to conquer spaces in networks like Bandeirantes, Record and Manchete, with simple program formulas, commercialized by themselves. The networks' vertical integration was not totally negative, though. Along the years, the networks gradually replaced importation with their own breed of programs, composing lineups radically different from the American ones (See Table 2). Building upon the strength of Brazilian radio, instead of cinema, the first television productions assumed most of the radio program formulas, as well as professionals.

Live comedy or music shows with simple sets and traditional radio hosts were transmitted from theaters and, since film equipment was still clumsy, news bulletins and imported materials were costly and hard to deal with. Paradoxically, the same factor of technology

Table 2 - Programming evolution in Brazil and United States

Brazil	United States
1950s	
• Telenovelas	• Variety shows
• Musicals	• News/ Information
• Variety shows	• Live drama
	• Westerns
	• Beginning of Situation Comedies (Sitcoms)
1960s	
Expansion brings low-brow	Success of one program generated similar
• Talk/variety shows	• Medical and lawyer programs
• Melodramatic style of radio soaps	• Sports
• Circus humour	• Feature movies (8 per week)
• Rites of folklore Performance	• News/ reality programs
1970s	
	Competition reduces innovation
	• Old sitcoms
	• Programs about crime
	• Mini-series
1980s	
	Recycle of old sitcoms, often zany, increasingly obsessed about sex, and dramas of the tracking, subduing, and killing of enemies foreign and domestic (Barnouw, 1990)
	• Reality shows substituted documentaries
	• Judicial programs
	• Panel shows attended by large studio audience and odd guests

Source: Compiled from the references indicated in the text.

development that allowed for more national production in the 1980s was responsible in the 1960s for more importation. Thanks to the videotape, program importation became simpler and cheaper, which caused a boom of foreign programs supported by many multinational advertisers, especially among the smaller TV stations. Recording shows in advance, Excelsior network introduced in the 1960s the concept of horizontal programming with the daily evening soap operas.

In the traditional vertical programming, still partly adopted by the American networks, there is a different program every day and, even if a program is repeated on a certain day of the week, the episodes are different and not connected. Horizontal programming means the transmission of the same program—the "telenovelas" (the Brazilian version of soap operas)—several days of the week, and it greatly promoted the habit of watching television among Brazilians. As television became popularized, however, the nationally produced programming was skewed towards the tastes of the lower classes that represent the largest proportion of the audience. As Straubhaar explains, "the lower class audiences are seem as having their own needs and identities, which tend to make them loyal to traditional, ethnic and regional cultures, which are often adapted to mass media" (Straubhaar, 1989). But the low-brow character of the overall programming did not mean low quality productions. On the contrary, as Globo consolidated its market leadership in the 1960s, it raised its production quality standard as a way to differentiate itself, while at the same time increasing the volume of necessary investment for entering the business (a barrier to entry). In the 1980s, its quality productions definitely conquered foreign markets, even though domestic competitors started to lure away the upper and lower classes, as Straubhaar (1989) comments:

> Although Globo ... seems to reach a very broad general audience, there is evidence that at both the upper and lower class ends of the television audience that interests and tastes diverge. Economics-based dependency theory predicts that the cultural interests and consumption habits of the 'bourgeoisie' will be increasingly internationalized, by virtue of the upper and upper middle classes' greater contact with foreign culture via travel, education, occupations, and their role in the international economic structure.

Thus, even though Brazilian television production had been growing strong with the introduction in the 1980s of independent producers and the SBT and Manchete networks, which respectively target the lower and upper classes, there was a demand for imported programming, especially among the upper classes. A quick look at the Brazilian television programming suggests that some of the programs best appreciated—after the telenovelas, of course—were those not produced nationally: feature films and action series. Not by mere chance, these were exactly the types of programs that the American cinema industry had mastered, and which constituted the bulk of the traditional importation of Brazilian television. But the hegemony of Globo as exporter and the American companies as providers of TV programs was increasingly challenged in the 1980s.

Besides Globo, Manchete and Bandeirantes started to export to other Latin American countries, looking forward to the implementation of the 1993 South Cone common market, which promised a larger business flow between the industries in Brazil, Argentina, Paraguay and Uruguay. The Brazilian product was not so easy to sell, however, as the American's. Produced on videotape, it was expensive and not as prestigious as the American film. As a heritage of its radio origins, the emotion and action is more present in the words, not in car pursuits and other easy gags, making it more difficult to understand (Bolaño, 1988). Melo points out that "exhibition rights for one Globo telenovela (comprising at least 120 chapters) cost about only one-third of those charged in the case of an American series (averaging 20 chapters)." Globo's initial sales to Latin America also indicated a low return rate due to high dubbing costs, reaching $150,000 for each telenovela (Melo, 1992).

Not only American feature films and action series for the upper classes hit the Brazilian market, but also some Latin American programs targeted at the lower classes. With the difficulties encountered in sustaining the production of its Mexican-style soap operas, SBT decided to import the real ones and reduce expenses while obtaining some sporadic audience hits, like the 21 percent share of "Carrossel" in 1991 (1991c). Melo reports that newcomer Brasil OM network similarly started to import telenovelas produced in Argentina, and SBT was ready to step into co-productions with the Mexican giant Televisa network (Melo, 1992). In fact, co-productions were increasingly becoming a good option for television companies around the world. With the recent changes in the American Fin-Syn Rules, described

127

in Chapter 3, the American networks received incentives to initiate co-productions with foreign companies, which were to become interesting investments for Brazilian entrepreneurs in the future. Up to that point, Globo had been the only Brazilian network to actively engage in various international co-productions, most of them directed to its foreign markets. Thanks to Globo's partial ownership of some European stations, like the Portuguese SIC and TeleMonteCarlo, it was able to easily exchange productions among the various markets. On the other hand, the American networks were also allowed into the international syndication market and the Brazilian networks were to find themselves flooded with old American series instead.

In the past, the American companies were more aggressive and quicker to act, transforming markets like Brazil into a secondary step to the exhibition of their programs. By the 1990s, the American movie productions were already going through a series of exhibition "windows" after they are launched. First, they are exhibited in the first-class theaters, then in the second class theaters and then they reach domestic television at the same time as they reach theaters worldwide. In the United States, the movies start in television at the pay-TV systems and VCRs, going to cable and regular broadcasters afterward. In the rest of the world, the movies tended to follow similar routes as each window is made available. The new Brazilian pay-TV represented a new window between the theaters and the broadcasters, attracting the attention of American companies but, in light of all such turnabout in the flux of programs, the future schedules of the new Brazilian channels would mainly depend on the companies' policies and hard to predict at that point.

Each company introduced the foreign programs under a different contract agreement with providers, but most of them kept some leeway to introduce or increase the proportion of nationally produced programs. Globo's pay-TV channels enjoyed a significant edge, being able to use the parent company's library and expertise. Already the service with the highest index of nationalization, GloboSat, assembled its own schedule, with programs coming from a variety of sources. Based on Globo's active international expansion, GloboSat was also fully expected to use its satellite coverage of Latin America to promote exportation to neighbor countries in the future. Since 1975, when

Globo first exported the telenovela "Gabriela" to Portugal, it learned the value of the international market. Melo indicates that:

> In 1977 Globo was already accounting for profits of $1million with the revenues of exported telenovelas; in 1985 these profits had increased to around $15 million; more recent profits have stabilized around the level of $20 million ... a modest amount [compared to] gross yearly sales revenues of $700 million (Melo, 1992).

Another form of program importation that could allow for an increased amount of local productions was adopted by Abril. Similarly to the Globo-Time/Life agreement in the 1960s, Abril signed a franchise agreement with the American MTV network to use its brand, programming and management expertise. As the American partner did not invest in the Brazilian channel and received only the payment of royalties, the deal did not attract any legal controversy. By acquiring a program package and balancing it with up to 50 percent of national productions, MTV-Abril was empowered to increase its production gradually. The same liberty was not as feasible for companies like TVA and PluralSat, which simply imported the satellite signal of foreign channels. For these channels, the insertion of local productions was conditioned to the inclusion of new channels or the end of the contract for a foreign 24-hour channel. The remainder of this chapter is a background on each of these new channels, with possible clues about their future (as seen from the perspective of a 1993 research witness!).

5.1 The new channels

Television segmentation started in Brazil with the advent of new concessions in some large metropolitan areas, like São Paulo. Since the VHF spectrum in such areas had already been taken, the ultra-high frequency was a compulsory choice. But the UHF that allowed for segmentation was not exactly new to the metro São Paulo region. Point-to-point UHF transmitters deliver network signals to affiliates in the countryside. Independent UHF stations, also recently built in the outskirts of the metro area, drop in their signal in the capital. This new market for independent stations offered them the chance to grow and, with them, the variety of programming offered besides that of the large networks. One of the first UHF stations to start broadcasting in the metro São Paulo area was TV ABC of Santo André (the "A" of three sister cities that include São Bernardo and São Caetano, in the vicinities of São Paulo city). Operating experimentally as early as July 1989, channel 40 initially reached only the so-called ABC region, with transmission power around ten kW. That was already a good beginning, considering that Santo Andre had 2.3 million inhabitants and figured among the ten cities with the highest acquisitive power per capita in the country (the first was São Caetano) (Pimenta, 1990).

The individual responsible for the station was 23-year-old Keynes Datto, son of Edson Danilo Datto, owner of the newspaper Diário do Grande ABC, three FM radio stations (at São Paulo, Ribeirão Preto and Curitiba) and one AM station (at São Bernardo do Campo) (1988d). The Dotto family invested about $150,000 intending to reach households of classes A, B and C with viewers older than 25 years (Pimenta, 1990), supposedly attending to the need of the region for regionalized media. Nevertheless, the bulk of its programming consisted of retransmitting the educational lineup of Funteve of Rio de Janeiro. ABC managers explained to the press that the plans were to start with transmissions of Funteve from 8 to 12:30 A.M., including, some day, local sports and news provided by the ABC newspaper journalism staff (Pimenta, 1990), reaching a maximum of 20 hours per week.

According to Ministerial Decree 93 of July 20, 1989, educational stations like ABC could generate their own programming, as long as it did not surpass 15 percent of the original broadcasting from the station to which it is affiliated (Fernandes, 1990). Production was very likely to be cost inefficient, though. Since the educational stations cannot sell slots to advertisers, the return on investments depends on special interest projects supported by private companies through the Sarney Law, which offers tax discounts to those investing in cultural promotions (1988b). While this region of São Paulo state, which encompasses the largest industrial plants of Brazil, still waited for its local television news, in 1990 São Paulo won its most important retransmitter of Funteve programming. At that moment, besides the 60 meter antenna tower on the highest point of Santo André, TV ABC also had a transmitter in downtown São Paulo. Another antenna 110 meters above the ground, was erected above a building on Avenida Paulista, in the same place where Scala FM radio, also owned by the Dotto family, operated. A $300,000 transmitter was also planned to increase the transmission power from ten kW to 316 kW (Pimenta, 1990).

Located in Guarulhos, another city of metropolitan São Paulo, channel 58 of Sistema Metropolitano de Rádio e Televisão started experimental operations in November 1989, a few months after TV ABC (1990g). Both stations retransmitted the programming of Funteve, under the same contract basis, but TV Metropolitana had been demonstrating a more aggressive entrepreneurship. When TV Metropolitana officially went on the air, in August 1990, it became the first UHF channel to be received by TV sets in São Paulo city (1990g). Its 1,000 Kw transmission covered a radius of 30-40 kilometers, reaching 3.5 million inhabitants in the eastern area of São Paulo city and approximately 900,000 living in Guarulhos, besides Osasco and Greater ABC regions (1991t). Like TV ABC, the majority of TV Metropolitana's programming came via satellite from TVE of Rio de Janeiro and was retransmitted between 8 and 1 A.M. But the local production time, restricted by contract to about 25 percent of the programming, had been gradually fulfilled by internal crews or by independent producers. Running Monday through Saturday at 7 P.M., the first local program was "Jornal Metropolitano," a 30-minute local news show produced by a staff of 15 journalists.

Following suit came "Quem Sabe Ganha" (a four-minute quiz show that ran three times a day with distribution of gifts over the telephone), "Domingo Musical" (a variety show with invited artists and contestants), "Top Clube" (a talk show with city personalities) and "Metropolitana Esporte" (a daily 15-minute news show that focused on the amateur sports in the city and was scheduled to transmit local soccer matches). Behind these initiatives were professionals with a variety of backgrounds, like Tony Auad, ex-host of wrestling shows and now commercial director; or Edi Newton, one of the pioneers of Brazilian television, with 30 years of work at Globo TV, who became the artistic director of Metropolitana (199It).

131

Just like ABC, Metropolitana was not allowed to sell advertising slots, but innovated by performing a barter deal with a local billboard company. It exchanged an outdoor with its promotional campaign for the production and transmission of a documentary on the use of outdoors. Metropolitana was also leading a campaign to demand from the government the right to sell slots. The law established that the educational stations could not sell slots because they already had the support of the government (1991v). However, since the owner, Jair Sanzoni, claimed not to have received any support from the government, he called the right to sell slots the right to survive (1991v). And he was a survivor. Jair Sanzoni owned the largest group of private radio stations in the country—16 radio stations (13 FM and two AM)—and had 29 other affiliates, besides eight educational TV stations in the main cities of the interior of São Paulo: Mogi das Cruzes (channel 49), Jundiaí (27), Taubaté (33), Campinas (10), Sorocaba (39), Osasco (48), São José dos Campos (25) and Guarulhos (58). Until the first quarter of 1991, however, only Mogi das Cruzes, Sorocaba and Guarulhos were operating. More recently, it was announced that TV Morada do Sol, channel 42 of Araraquara, was planning to reach São Paulo, with a power of 100 kW. The director, Roberto Montoro Filho, indicated a programming focused on news, Northern music (sertaneja) and specials about agriculture and cattle.

5.2 The Niche Channels

Jovem Pan and MTV-Abril promoted a big revolution in the Brazilian television industry by introducing the concept of segmented channels. For the first time, a channel concentrated on offering only one kind of programming for a certain niche of the market. Like all pioneer experiences, the history of their first days was full of setbacks and innovative solutions to new and old problems. In essence, they had to identify a market demand not fully or properly serviced by the existing networks—Abril found rock music and Jovem Pan found news. Then they had to measure this segment of the market and define its potential, both in numerical terms and acquisitive power. If there were enough potential viewers and advertisers, the new stations went on to develop or buy programming that would service the specific demands of their audience. Another contemporary concession never came off the ground. The UHF channel 53 of São Paulo, conceded to Fundação Evangélica Trindade, was scheduled to start operating on July 1, 1990, according to commercial director Gidalti Alencar. While its programming focus was never known, it was said to be applying for an increase in transmission power, from 1 kW to about 100 kW (Fernandes, 1990). Here are some of these "niche channel" experiences, as recollected through a series of hundreds of newspaper clippings.

5.2.1 Yes, We Have MTV!

It was more than a decade earlier that the Abril Group, founded in the early fifties by two Italian-Americans, started making plans to become a real communication conglomerate. From its printing plant— the largest in Latin America—comes about 120 magazines and several telephone directories, among other publications, which qualified Abril as one of the most important media companies of Brazil. The expansion of the group towards the electronic media was, therefore, supposed to be the next step of its consolidation in the market, following the example of Globo Network, which started as an offspring of O Globo newspaper. Under the close scrutiny of the government, however, the television industry always posed strong barriers to the entry of groups not totally aligned with the government's interests. The first opportunity for Abril appeared after 1980, when the government dismembered the pioneer TV Tupi. After numerous political, besides business negotiations, Abril was passed over in favor of the Silvio Santos Group and Bloch Publishing Group. In 1985, when Silvio Santos was pressured to sell his share of TV Record, Abril was again considered by the press as the best bidder.

For reasons yet to be properly explained, however, the deal failed to come to terms. Abril started pursuing different strategies. Abril Video, an independent video producer created a few years before, bought time at TV Bandeirantes and, later, at Gazeta to air its journalistic programs. In spite of the low ratings, the programs enjoyed a reputation for innovative and critical journalism. This latter characteristic (criticism) could have bothered enough political figures to seal the end of the programs in 1987. The next year, Abril Video withdrew from broadcasting television, repositioning itself in the growing home-video market as both a producer and distributor (1989a). In 1985, the government opened the bidding for concessions of new UHF transmitter stations in São Paulo city. And on this front Abril finally succeeded, beating other powerful media groups for the concession of channel 32. Six years later, Abril's video and TV companies (Abril Video[8], TVAbril/ MTV and TVA), headed by the founder's grandsons, were already responsible for 6.2 percent of the conglomerate's profits (See Table 3), with forecasts that this percentage would rise to about 35 percent in four years (Blecher, 1991).

Table 3 - Abril Group - Profits per Area 1991

Division	Percentage
TV/Video*	6.2
Publications Distribution	6.5
Printing	11.5
Telephone Directories	19.0
Magazines	56.8

Source: Blecher, Nelson. "Televisão muda o perfil do Grupo Abril". Folha de S. Paulo. September 13, 1991.

Meanwhile, the challenge was still to amortize Abril's huge initial investments. Channel 32 consumed investments of $15 million just before inauguration--$10 million on equipment alone (See Table 4). That included 4,300 square meters for three central studios, a mobile studio and six mobile units (Regina, 1990). Another $400,000 were spent on computer equipment; a system based on PCs was responsible for the programming of the station. The Automatic Cartridge Recorder controlled the insertion of 256 videotapes, with 30 minutes each, maintaining the station on the air for 125 hours without help (Lachtermacher, 1991).

8   In 1991, Abril Video sold almost a million prerecorded tapes to rental stores.

Table 4 - TV Abril's equipment

Equipment	Nationality	Brand
Antenna	French	Thomson
Transmitters	American	Comark
Cameras	German	Philips
Digital Effects	American	Ampex
Maintenance Equip.	American	Tektronix
Computer Graphics	Canadian	Alias
Graphic Station		Silicon Graphics
Personal Iris		
Paint System		Ampex Visual Arts

Source: (Fernandes, 1990)

It was only much later that Roger Karman, Abril's Vice-President for TV/Video, confessed early plans to have a programming either centered in journalism or aimed at the female public, using the successful experiences of their magazines (Sayão, 1990). Past experiences in these niches were, nevertheless, very negative. Abril's "Olhar Eletrônico," aired by Gazeta, and Globo's "TV Mulher" (TV Woman) were marked by low ratings and short life spans. The mystery surrounding Abril's programming was removed on March 7, 1990, with the official launching of "MTV Brasil" in São Paulo city. Abril, whose magazines had already surveyed and identified the young public as an attractive market, was probably more than interested when Gazeta turned down a $2 million Music Television (MTV) programming package (Pimenta, 1990). After successfully translating such well-known American trademarks as "Playboy," "Cosmopolitan" and "Disney," Abril managed to get even more than programs from MTV. The five-year renewable contract brought to Abril the technical and management know-how of MTV as well, raising inevitable comparisons with the Globo/Time-Life agreement in the 1960s. Like the Time-Life/TV Globo contract, the participation of the American partner included decisions such as which commercials could be accepted, but the contract did not involve investments from the American MTV. And instead of shares in the profits of the Brazilian

135

channel, MTV payments after the contract fee consisted of royalties for the use of its brand—all legal practices under the Brazilian laws (Regina, 1990).

Present in 38 countries (See Table 5), MTV expansion into Brazil soon presented some local twists to the American long-planned corporate strategies. The videoclips coming from different MTVs all around the world were exclusive to Abril for a period of one to three months, and the Brazilian videoclips could also be retransmitted in the other countries (Gaspar, 1991). There were just not enough national videoclips, nor rock stars, to fulfill even half of the primetime (7 to 10 P.M.), which the law required to be Brazilian productions. MTV-Abril's premiere at midday on October 20, 1990 (Blecher, 1991) was marked by 70 percent imported programming (Alencar, 1990). By March 1991, when the law promoting Brazilian-produced programming was abolished, Abril had produced by itself twenty videoclips, with unit prices evaluated between $20,000 and $30,000. That meant almost one clip for each furnished by the national record companies (1991). Using film instead of videotape, Abril was the only MTV network in the world to produce videoclips (Gaspar, 1991).

According to Abril officials, this kind of production was practically restricted to Globo TV, which transmitted an average of two foreign and two internally produced videoclips every Sunday night. To break the dependence on Globo, Abril had to find new human resources. Foreign directors and Brazilian movie professionals were contracted to produce clips and, to diversify from the limited artistic base on the national scene, the program "Demo MTV" was created with the task of discovering new music groups and talents (Gaspar, 1991). Besides videoclips, Abril was also pushed into the production of commercials, since they had to follow the characteristics of the programming, as defined by American MTV. These efforts paid off. Abril gained the respect of the radio stations, which were playing more MTV-selected songs, and of the record companies, which consulted Abril when deciding which song of a long-play record should become a videoclip (Gaspar, 1991). By the time of the start of this study, in January 1992, the proportion of national materials had been raised to 50 percent and Abril staff proudly talked about how impressed the MTV consultants were during their last inspection visit.

Table 5 - MTV in other countries

MTV Europe
Launched on August 1, 1987.
A partnership between Maxwell Entertainment Group and Viacom International, Inc., the network currently reaches 20.4 million households in 25 countries, 24 hours a day, by satellite, cable and terrestrial distribution. It acquires its own videoclips, drawing from the domestic markets in individual countries, to discover non-English and American bands making an international sound. MTV Europe is an English-language network.

MTV Japan
Originally launched on October 1, 1984, through a licensing agreement with Asahi Broadcasting Corp., MTV was seen four hours a week for four years. On July 4, 1988, MTV was launched 5.5 hours a week on the Tokyo Broadcasting System, Inc.(TBS), through a licensing agreement. TBS is the largest commercial broadcasting station in Japan and reaches 13.5 million households in the metro Tokyo area. MTV Japan is a Japanese language network.

MTV Australia
Launched on April 16, 1987.
Seen live 5.5 hours per week on The Nine Network, ranked number one across Australia, the network reaches over seven million homes. MTV Australia is an English-language network.

MTV International
Launched on July 15, 1988.
Seen in the United States and other countries throughout Latin America (Aruba, Argentina, Bolivia, Chile, Costa Rica, Honduras, Mexico, Panama and Paraguay), reaching 10.2 million households. In the U.S. it is distributed by Telemundo Network and in Latin America by MTV Networks Syndication Sales Worldwide. It is a weekly one-hour program, on broadcast television, including Spanish and English videos. MTV International is a Spanish-language program.

Source: U.S. MTV's press releases

The record companies assumed the budget and the choice of directors, while Abril had become a sporadic co-producer. The average productions rarely exceeded $30,000, while the specials reached a maximum of $60,000—a humble figure compared to Michael Jackson's $4 million (1992). But Abril offered more than videoclips (See Table 6). Programming was composed of music (65 percent), sports, humor and journalism aimed at a 12- to 34-year-old public. Surfing and roller-skating were the main sports covered and each hour a three minute arts and entertainment news bulletin was inserted (Regina, 1990). Like American MTV, Abril adopted a single segment marketing concentration, balancing the risks of being the first targeted television channel in Brazil with the high attractiveness of the market. Some early surveys detected that the people within the MTV age segment were heavier consumers of several products, like beverages, fashion, etc. Even though the videoclips did not exactly abound in Brazilian television, there were signs that a young group with high acquisitive power already knew the MTV concept, either through American movies and music or through tapes recorded in the United States by traveling friends. On the other hand, this segment's attention and loyalty had been traditionally the hardest one to conquer and maintain. The teenagers, in particular, have a more unstable profile and are less exposed to the media. The advertisers knew such odds, and Abril was faced with a triple challenge: expand signal reception in already congested markets, increase general public awareness and lure advertisers to the new segmentation concept.

MTV-Abril started with a restored building which once was the headquarters of TV Tupi, the first television station in the country. Its 143-meter antenna had an irradiation power of 1,000 kW (Department, 1990), reaching a radius of 100 kilometers in metro São Paulo (Regina, 1990). Initially, the broadcasting was restricted to 13 hours, Sunday

Table 6 - MTV-Abril programming of all times

Program	Schedule	Description
MTV no ar	daily - 7:30 to 8 PM	news of music world
Disk MTV	workdays, 6 to 7:30 PM	10 videoclips more asked by audience during the day, besides 12 segments, including "Invasão de domicílio" in which the host interviews singers in their houses
TV Zona	Wednesday - 9 to 10 PM	singer Rita Lee performs and presents videoclips
Netos do Amaral		comedian Marcelo Tas revisits the places reporter Amaral Neto showed in his weekly program in the 1970s
Video Music	12 PM	Video-jockey (VJ) Cuca hosts videoclips only

Program	Schedule	Description
Clássicos MTV		VJ Rodrigo presents old classic videoclips
Top 10		VJ Luiz Thunderbird presents the 10 most requested videoclips in USA
Semana Rock	Saturdays	Zeca Camargo does interviews and music news
Dance MTV		VJ Maria Paula presents music to dance
Lado B		VJ Luiz Thunderbird presents new songs by local independent groups
Rockstória	Sundays	interviews and retrospectives
Top 20 Brasil		VJ Astrid Fontenelle presents the 20 most requested videoclips in Brazil
Cine MTV		interviews and critics of movies
Tutti&Dani	weekdays- 11AM to 1 PM weekends 1:30 to 4 PM	VJ Daniela Barbieri presents the music hits of the FM radios
Gás Total	weekdays 4 to 6:45 PM	VJ Gastão hosts heavy metal music
Beat MTV	weekdays 9 to 10:30 PM	VJ Maria Paula shows new tendencies and rhythms
Check Up	Sundays 9:30 to 10:30 PM	VJ Maria Paula hosts a restrospective of the career of invited artists
121	Saturdays 12:30 to 3 AM	VJ Thunderbird hosts less famous bands
Yo! MTV Raps		
Mastermix		
Top 10 EUA		
Fúria Metal		

• Zue, with Astrid Fontenele, starts with two hours of videoclips, in the place of VideoMusic, presented by Otaviano.
• At 2 P.M., MTV-pix brings the clips most frequently played in Europe and USA. VJ Cuca presents it, leaving "Non Stop."
• Every night, from 8 to 9:30PM, Megamax, with Maria Paula, substitutes Furia, with Gastao. It corresponds to the programming of American VH-I channel, aimed at a more adult public (27+).
• Every weeknight, from IIP.M. to IA.M., VJ Thunderbird presents "Rock-Blocks," with vanguard rock.
• "Big-Vid" starts every weekend morning, with Otaviano presenting the best clips of all times (Lazaretti, 1992).

Source: Compiled by author from several MTV promotional materials.

through Thursday, extending to 16 hours on Fridays and Saturdays. A 24-hour schedule was planned to be implemented only after two years, but a gradual increase of hours had been taking place toward a round-the-clock channel. The expectation was to reach at least one percent of the four million TV households of metro São Paulo (Regina, 1990), and the expansion previewed for the first year included 30 million people in 22 municipalities. Through 1995 the forecast was to reach 50 million people in 50 cities (Department, 1990), completely returning investments that were quickly exceeding the $20 million figure. The planned network, with 30 retransmission stations, was not intended to be an extensive network, but was planned to cover selected parts of the country (Martinho, 1990), which had not kept Abril from a quick expansion (See Table 7).

Table 7 - MTV Channels in Brazil

City	State	Channel
São Paulo	São Paulo	32
Porto Alegre	Rio Grande do Sul	24
Recife	Pernambuco	27
Manaus	Amazonas	23
São Luis	Maranhão	18
Rio de Janeiro	Rio de Janeiro	24
Porto Velho	Roraima	25
Macapá	Amapá	24
Sorocaba*	São Paulo	18
Novo Hamburgo*	Rio Grande do Sul	18

* These cities are not capitals of the state.

Source: MTV-Abril's advertising on VejaSP magazine of August 17, 1992.

Since June 8, 1990, Abril had leased channel 4A1, transponder frequency 3830 MHz (Sayão, 1990) of BrasilSat II. The first dolby stereo signal on the Brazilian satellite (Netto, 1990) cost Abril $1.3 million a year (Martinho, 1990), but allowed reception in at least 10 other cities in the first year of operations (1991z). Most of the stations captured the signal from the satellite and retransmitted it at the UHF frequency. That was the case of MTV Porto Alegre, which started operating at October 7, 1991 on UHF channel 24, reaching 15 cities in Rio Grande do Sul state, at the extreme south of Brazil. The $200,000 initial investment was partially financed by six founding sponsors— Pepsi (soft drinks), Colgate (chemicals), Nike and US Top (clothing), Cashmere Bouquet (deodorants) and Lacesa (dairy)—paying $45,000 (1991k).

In Rio de Janeiro, the case was different. On August 17, 1990, Abril signed a three-year contract with TV Corcovado, VHF channel 9. By this contract the station started producing and airing MTV-like programs to an expected audience of 1.8 million people between 15 and 39 years old (Xexeo, 1990), and shared the revenues with Abril. That was a radical programming change for TV Corcovado, which used to be filled with paid programs by religious groups (Silva, 1990). In 1991 the Corcovado station was bought by state senator Jose Carlos Martinez. The press reported the purchase as part of President Collor's political strategy of having supporting media in each state for the next presidential elections. The $1 million-per-month contract between Abril and Guilherme Stoliar—main shareholder of Corcovado and also vice-president of SBT Network—terminated in October 1991, but had an extension of 6 months, in case any of the parties decided not to have it renewed (Lobo, 1991). In February 1992, MTV-Abril returned to Rio on UHF channel 24. To make people tune in to these new channels, Abril invested $1.5 million in advertising for the launching, a campaign entitled *"Yes,* We Have MTV!" (Regina, 1990). But when it transmitted its first image—a welcome clip to the audience—the initial results were far from rewarding (1990c). The first day of MTV-Abril in São Paulo was full of problems due to mistakes in the software on the computer that controls the insertion of programs. Bad cuts, long periods of black screen and confusion in the insertion of vignettes were the first hints that something was wrong. In spite of the calls during the day, "Cine MTV" and "Saturday Night Live," respectively at 4 and 9:30 P.M., were simply not transmitted (1990c). The first day in Rio was even worse. TV Corcovado premiered without any sound. And when the problem was detected, it arbitrarily played remaining like this for a full hour (Xexeo, 1990).

In March 1991, after six months of transmission, an IBOPE survey indicated that 17 percent of respondents from São Paulo and 27 percent from Rio had watched MTV-Abril (1991e). Nevertheless, American consultation on programming was seemingly not achieving many positive points, as other surveys revealed many critics. The video-jockeys (VJs), for example, were criticized for a false intimacy, for using old slang and for moving too much on the screen (1990c). After a month of operation, Abril changed the programming. The plan was to introduce live shows and move some late-night shows to earlier hours. Programs like "Yo! MTV Raps" on Mondays at 1 A.M. and "Fúria Metal" (heavy metal) on Fridays at 2 P.M. were hardly watched, while there was criticism that there was too much repetition of clips during the day (Flesch, 1990). It was in the commercialization process that the MTV know-how really made a difference for Abril. With the support of consecutive surveys and unorthodox audience promotions, Abril raised the number of advertisers from 23 at the premiere to 153 one year later (Sá, 1991). Actually, before its premiere, Abril already had five founder-advertisers: Bamerindus (bank), Philips (electronics), São Paulo Alpargatas (clothing), Nestle (food) and Brahma (beverages). All signed contracts to invest $864,000 each in advertising within six months (Marques, 1991). In September 1990, the advertising space started to be sold, and the expectation was to get $2.3 million by the end of the year, but the real profits were $3.5 million. Advertising at Abril did not surpass the limit of eight minutes per hour, almost half of the time of the regular networks. The length of the spot was not rigid, varying from a few seconds to a minute or more. An insertion of 30 seconds cost $530 in August 1991 (Lobo, 1991), and the revenues for that year were expected to be $10 million (Marques, 1991), although the economic crisis of Brazil did not help.

In fact, in the beginning of 1991, while the regular networks counted revenues 40 to 50 percent below their expectations, Abril was only 30 percent below (Gaspar, 1991). Their secret of success was tied to convincing the advertisers that Abril could reach their target market better than the other networks. Since the UHF channels were not included in the regular audience survey services of institutions like IBOPE, Abril had to produce its own convincing that going to a fast-food restaurant was the most common practice among youngsters—after listening to music—large fast-food chains were convinced to advertise on MTV. Other surveys indicated that MTV's typical viewers were from class A and B, with high acquisitive power and personal income, constituting a market that consumed eight million sneakers and 35 million pairs of jeans every year (Lobo, 1991). Until April 1991, when Abril audience ratings started to be part of IBOPE regular reports (1991e), the phone calls received by the program "Disk MTV" were also used to evaluate public reception (Flesch, 1990). The average viewership in Rio, where the VHF transmissions were included in the IBOPE measurements, was one percent, with peaks of three percent in events like the ten years of MTV (Lazaretti, 1992).

Since the inclusion of UHF stations in the IBOPE People Meter in September 1991, the average audience index had been one to two points in São Paulo (Gaspar, 1991). Like American MTV, Abril offered several promotions involving the audience and pop artists. The lists of entrants in every promotion become high-valued mailing lists to the clients and Abril, which accumulated more than 100,000 of these leads (prospective consumers) (Lobo, 1991). The winner of the first promotion had a dinner with Paul McCartney in London (Flesch, 1990). Another promotion involved three sponsors and two supporting newspapers taking the selected winner to the 1991 Video Music Awards in Los Angeles (Lobo, 1991). The Nike brand, licensed by Alpargatas in Brazil, invested $70,000 in a one-minute TV spot transmitted exclusively by MTV, besides a six-month exclusive sponsorship of "Top 20 Brasil," one of the most popular programs. The selected letter that contained five of the most frequently played clips won a tape of them, plus a pair of Nike shoes (1991m). More extraordinarily, Philips sponsored a promotion in which the winner received Philips' most complete sound system and a weekend to listen to it very loudly, while the parents won a trip to Águas de Lindóia, a peaceful resort (Marques, 1991).

At the time this study was conducted, in January 1992, the impression was that Abril was still adapting MTV programming to the Brazilian tastes, including some videoclips fromVH-1, MTV's channel directed to older audiences in America. For example, a survey by the Sinal agency made in December 1991 with 1,400 youngsters in São Paulo and Rio de Janeiro from classes A, B and C indicated:

- 80 percent of the audience thinks MTV's programming is addressed to them and the same proportion approves it.

- The medium viewer is 12 to 19 years old, from classes A/B.

- The heavy viewer, who watches MTV five to seven days a week, is male. Four in ten are between 15 and 19 years old and six in ten are from classes A/B.

- Rock is the most preferred overall and rap is more listened to by boys in São Paulo (34 percent). Next is heavy metal, also appreciated more by males (29 percent in SP and 28 percent in Rio).

- Surprisingly, Brazilian popular music—which was not present in MTV—also got fans: the girls in Rio (58 %) , followed by the girls in São Paulo (49 percent) (Lazaretti,1992).

5.2.2 Jovem Pan - Is the dream over?

After a frustrated application in 1983, when it lost to Abril, Televisão Jovem Pan was granted license number 101 in 1987, beating out larger media conglomerates, like Jornal do Brasil, Visão, Rádio Jornal de São Paulo/TV Bandeirantes, TV3/ Editora Três, SuperTupi and Diário do Grande ABC. The success of the application can be attributed, to a large extent, to the high credibility and respect gained by AM radio station Jovem Pan-1 (620 KHz), also owned by one of the partners of the TV station (which inherited the name). The strong and nimble journalism that characterized the radio station—and that was planned for transplantation to the TV station—classified this station as one of the most respected radio stations in São Paulo. Still, the sum of brief moments of attention dedicated by Jovem Pan audience to its news bulletins were not enough to provide any significant audience ratings in any given survey. The advertisers considered it a mandatory radio station buy, even though the station's prices were the highest in the market, but translating that to TV was not a sure thing (Nunes, 1987). On January 20, 1988 Jovem Pan (JP) signed the contract for a 15-year license to operate UHF channel 16 of open reception (Maiello,

1988). JP was considered by some as the first company to study the viability of subscription television in Brazil in the beginning of the 1980s, but its option for the free delivery of signals may be a symbol of its disbelief in the consolidation of such a system in the country (Demarchi, 1990). The contract fixed in six months the time for the company to present the technical plans and two years to put it on the air (Maiello, 1988). JP barely made it. Many setbacks delayed the initial operations, forcing Jovem Pan to abandon its plans of being the first UHF station to broadcast in the capital. The rush for primacy also had a technical reason. JP technicians were convinced that the public would align their new UHF antennas to the first transmitters available and that late comers would have few choices but to place transmitters close to the ones already in operation.

The first problem the technical director, José Olímpio Franco, had to face was the delay in the importation process of the $8 million worth of equipment he bought in the United States from well-recognized manufacturers, like Sony and Bosh-Philips. When the equipment finally arrived, in late 1990, Jovem Pan was ready to set up an impressive journalism machine. Planned to operate in the same mode as its radio counterpart, JP-TV's electronic news gathering would allow journalists to count on nine mobile units, besides helicopter, to cover the city. The news as sent by microwave to automatic-tuning memory antennas at Avenida Paulista, Barra Funda's headquarters in the city, or at Jaraguá Peak outside it. For special events, a bus was converted into a mobile studio. Eight cameras, post-production and broadcasting capacity enabled the bus to maintain the station on air by itself. The quality of the images was assured by 36 digital Betacam video cameras with professional videotape recorders that operated in NTSC with metal Beta tapes (1/2 inches). After passing through one of the 12 editing tables available, the news bulletins would go to post production and preparation of master tapes, performed by three new D2 tape format machines.

The Pen System, which allows the coloring of pictures on the screen, a still images databank and a Digital Video Effects computer were responsible for quality vignettes. And a Betacard Computerized Insertion System automatically controlled the insertion of commercials (Giannini, 1989). Experimental broadcasting started on November 29,

145

1990 for 12 hours a day, during economic reforms implemented by President Fernando Collar, who had assumed the position two weeks before. The official start, scheduled for March 1991, was again delayed for another 60 days, hoping for the best. It was the beginning of one of the largest economic crises in Brazilian history, and Jovem Pan had invested, by then, a total of $16 million. About $5 million were spent on the basic infrastructure alone (Nunes, 1987). JP bought a 3,850 square-meter lot of land in a central part of São Paulo (240 Várzea Street, Barra Funda neighborhood) and built a monumental 4,000-square-meter (built area) headquarters, designed to hold the studios, transmission center and administrative offices. The larger studio, with 500 square meters, was to be used for the production of journalism programs, while the other two were for post-production activities.

Still looking for a strategic position for its transmitter, JP invested more to have an antenna in one of the highest and most expensive places in the center of the city, where many other broadcasters' antennas were also located. An 88-ton antenna tower was erected over Senai (Industry National Service) building at Avenida Paulista, which was remodeled to support it. Approximately 200 meters above the ground, the antenna had the same height as the TV Globo's antenna—for years, one of the most recognized of the city's "landmarks," supported by the Gazeta building, practically beside it. The 20-meter antenna built by Dieletric Communications had a power of 1,000 KW, and the stereo transmission reached a radius of 50 kilometers, servicing metro São Paulo or the equivalent of 60 municipalities. The eliptic polarization that characterizes such antennas facilitated the reception by indoor antennas, which were predominant in São Paulo (Giannini, 1989). Until the end of February 1992, the antenna had cost JP about Cr$780 million ($780,000 in January), which were to be paid through the production and transmission of twenty institutional videos for Senai.

By the end of the two-month delay period, a huge recession had definitely taken over the country. Old barter contracts, which financed more than $3.5 million for Jovem Pan, stood as testimony of the strong interest by the advertisers in the new channel. Companies like Pirelli (cables), Ford (cars), Hobjeto (furniture), Olivetti, Philco-Hitachi, Philips (electronics), and Concrelix (construction), for example, guaranteed their commercial spots very early, in exchange for equipment and materials. However, many of the advertisers that Jovem Pan expected to help finance its official start were scared away at that time. Without much financial slack, the plans to deliver sports, journalism and service information—and eventually to add feature films and clips—were far from becoming true, in spite of the effort of JP' s executives (Demarchi, 1990). Narciso Kalili, Journalism Director since November 1990, had designed operations to transform JP into a Brazilian equivalent of CNN (Cable News Network). Programming was to be divided into long blocks, with news, debates and entertainment, with a bulletin of ongoing news and service information every half hour, all coordinated by anchors—a figure not common to Brazilian news yet. On weekends, the sports were to be featured and JP already purchased exclusivity rights for the transmission of the Argentine soccer championships.

The ex-chief director of special reports for Globo Network had plans to initially hire 200 people for the production of journalism programs, increasing staff to 500 as the broadcasting period reaches 24 hours (Anderaos, 1991a). On the commercial side, Vice-president Marcelo Mainardi planned to attract advertisers like Rhodia, Gessy Lever (chemicals), Itaú, Bradesco and Unibanco (banks), with approximately thirty different formats to run their advertising. And if such an eclectic policy was not convincing, specific packages could be negotiated to better reach JP's audience of older men from classes A, B and C (Demarchi, 1990). Even though its infrastructure was ready, Jovem Pan was being forced to maintain a minimum group of eight to ten people, broadcasting a programming with zero cost, based on movies received from embassies and soccer games whose rights it had already paid for. A few months before the deadline legally imposed for its official start in September, the need for capital injection was clear and the original partners—Objetivo Schools' João Carlos Di Gênio (30 percent) JP radio's Antonio Augusto Amaral de Carvalho (30 percent), and Fernando Vieira de Melo (40 percent)—sought new money.

Indústria Brasileira de Formulários (IBF) bought Melo's 40 percent in a $10-million transaction in July 1991. The buyout, however, was not as welcome as it seems. For many years, the JP radio station had used the slogan "Jovem Pan is only radio" to demonstrate that it was not conditioned to any other interest but radio diffusion. The slogan was also a critique of the communication oligarchies of the country, which were compromised by other business interests (Nunes, 1987). Nevertheless, the press had repeatedly denounced the connection betweem IBF and political interests. With a profit of $170 million in 1990, IBF group comprised 14 companies in the printing industry that specialized in the production of computer continuous-feed paper, check books, air tickets and instant lottery cards. In the previous six years, IBF, which took 42 years since its foundation in 1943 to incorporate eight companies, managed to buy five companies and to create a sixth. In January 1991 it bought DCI Group, the ninth in the list of largest national journalistic companies, for cash. Such incredible buying capacity started rumors in the market that political groups could be using IBF as a front (Chaim, 1991). The rumors were also based on a 1988 scandal involving the company and the ex-governor of São Paulo, Orestes Quércia. The governor was accused of favoring the company in the competition for providing the instant lottery cards and, considering his interest in media companies—he owned directly and indirectly three television stations, four newspapers, a magazine and three radio stations in the main cities of the state—it seemed reasonable to think that IBF and JP could help him be elected in the next presidential elections (1991f).

Jovem Pan's regular broadcasting started on July 2, 1991 with 16 hours a day—just enough not to lose its license. Even though it was going to keep its coverage restricted for a while to São Paulo city, JP had been active in the war for rebroadcasting affiliates in the interior of the state. By the first months of 1992, engineer Lucrécia de Fátima Costa counted ten stations with contracts to rebroadcast signals and about 60 others were in preparation to do so (1992 interview). Some news segments were scheduled for production in Rio de Janeiro and Brasília, and the transmission could reach the whole country through JP's full transponder in Brasilsat II. International news was provided through a subscription to CNN services, but there were future plans to employ correspondents in some of the less conventional places, like Berlin and Peking (Anderaos, 1991a). In spite of its potential for success, Jovem Pan's future was still hard to predict. Without a definition of its programming, and running many hours of short Japanese documentaries, JP's audience rating barely reached a half point during any time on any day. Much of the equipment remained untouched in its boxes and only four programs had been produced: Jornal São Paulo (news), No pique da Pan (sports news), Parada Obrigatória (interviews) and Super VHS (video technology).

With monthly losses amounting to $500,000, JP had quickly consumed more than $30 million from the pockets of its three owners, who did not seem to be able to come to any agreement. In spite of their old friendship, Antonio Augusto Amaral de Carvalho (better known as "Tuta") owner of Jovem Pan radio, and João Carlos Di Genio, owner of Objetivo Schools had a fight in 1991 and stopped talking to each other. Tuta had not been to the company's building since December 5, 1991, and many articles reported him out of the company, even though his 30 percent shares had not been sold (Luz, 1992). One of the pioneers of the live transmission of sports, Tuta was considered by JP's employees as the spirit behind the whole project. After all, Tuta produced and directed many hits during his 20 years at TV Record of São Paulo, when this network was the audience leader (Nunes, 1987). In 1972, after winning 11 "Roquete Pinto" trophies (something equivalent to an American Emmy's) and many "Governador do Estado Awards," he bought Jovem Pan radio from his brothers and made it a success (Maiello, 1988). While all three partners confess to be trying to sell their shares, Globo TV offered to buy the immense headquarters of JP-TV. The fate of the "Brazilian CNN" was dependent on its owners' disposition and history showed it was not a good one.

5.2.3 Luqui - May play someday

More than a year after receiving its concession, the premiere of UHF channel 21 of São Paulo city was still uncertain by mid-1992. Its plans, however, had been long exalted by the press. The history of what was supposed to be the first all-sports channel of Brazil was also the history of Luciano do Vale, narrator of three soccer World Cups, 74 Formula One races, and main sports presenter of Globo TV in the 1970s. In 1981 he left Globo and in 1982 he founded his own company Luqui—in association with his long-time colleague Francisco Leal Filho (known as "Quico"). His idea was to create a sports programming package to be sold to any channel, following the syndication example of American television. Record was the first network to be interested, but there was never an agreement. Bandeirantes then offered a consortium operation in which Luqui used Bandeirantes equipment and broadcasting time, managing the production and commercialization, while the profits were equally divided. It was a tough deal for Luqui, one that had to overcome the overall low investments in the sector and popular unawareness of other sports besides soccer.

But with vibrant narration, Luciano managed to popularize volleyball in 1982, initiating the public to a whole diversification of sports. When the sports events were not there to be broadcast, Luqui promoted the events by itself. That was the case with the heavy-weight boxer Maguila, coached by Luciano, and with the Senior Soccer Cup, which he organized while simultaneously working as coach for the Brazilian team. The initial 14 weekly hours of programming on Bandeirantes reached 20 hours in 1990 and kept expanding. With an average audience twice the size of the normal programs produced by Bandeirantes TV and peaks of 25 points, Luqui became vital to the network, whose new slogan changed to "the sports channel." By the time the new UHF channels started to be distributed, Luqui already had 273 employees and, while Luciano had been an informal adviser for Bandeirantes TV for eight years, the network was feeling the pressure to give him a more proper position in the organization. Thus, an arrangement was made. Bandeirantes had traditionally maintained tempestuous relationships with the government and would hardly stand a chance to win a UHF concession, but Luciano and Luqui had no political past. Luciano also had casually come to know the son of ex-president Sarney, who recommended that he apply for a concession (Xavier Filho, 1991). In 1990, the just-created company LQB (Luqui-Bandeirantes) won the concession and set the premiere day for December 21, later postponing to May 13, 1991, the date Bandeirantes TV commemorated 24 years with a new antenna at Avenida Paulista (1990d). It was planned to initially have eight hours of programming, quickly expanding to 12 hours, from 2 P.M. to 2 A.M. A 24-hour schedule was supposed to come within six months (1990d).

Since June 11, 1991, however, Luciano and Quico assumed positions at Bandeirantes, leaving questions about whether channel 21 would ever go on the air. Theoretically, Luciano explained that his company's association with Bandeirantes would follow a strategy used by the American ABC and ESPN networks. The UHF channel would present all phases of a tournament, creating the public interest for the subject, while the coverage of the last phase would be made by Bandeirantes (Xavier Filho, 1991). The investment anticipated was from $10-15 million (Fernandes, 1990) to have transmitter power of 1.5 MW, sending the signal to all of metro São Paulo and even to some other important cities in the interior of the state (1990d). Luciano announced a programming based on journalism, sports and movies, aiming at the family and avoiding scenes of sex and violence (Xavier Filho, 1991). He planned to include one hour of educational sports programs, with famous athletes teaching the basic techniques of each sport and sponsors providing special didactic books with exercises. About 40 percent of the programming was to be national, presented by an all-female staff, of various races, in contrast with the other channels (1990d). And, contrary to the ESPN lineup offered by TVA, LQB promised to cover sports that were more popular in Brazil. In order of preference, they listed soccer, Formula One car racing, volleyball, basketball, tennis and swimming (Pimenta, 1990). The events already contracted to be broadcast offered an idea of what was to come: Italian Soccer Cup, NBA basketball, National Soccer Tournament, Indy Formula racing and Luqui's Pelé Cup of senior soccer players (1990d).

Despite all the best laid plans, the station was never to be.

5.3 The pay-TV channels

In 1988, bulletin number 90 of the Brazilian Ministry of Communications established March 24, of the next year as the date to start receiving the applications for four new UHF channels in the metropolitan area of São Paulo. It was the official beginning of pay television in Brazil. By August of 1989, President José Sarney named the winners: the largest graphic company in Latin America, Abril Publications; the largest television company in the country, Globo Network; Walter Fontoura, then director of O Globo newspaper; and Showtime, a company connected to Mathias Machline. Actual operations, however, preceded regulation and KeyTV, which started operating in 1988, had been considered a pioneer pay-TV system in the country (Hoineff, 1991). Transmitting horse races through Brasilsat to ten subscribers—mostly horse owners—and for the Jockey Clubs of São Paulo and Rio de Janeiro, which redistributed the images by UHF or cable to more than 200 betting places. KeyTV was more a closed-circuit system than a real pay-TV. Owner of Sharp Brasil, Sid Informática (computers) and Digibanco (bank automation equipment), Machline was also a well-known personal friend of Sarney and his channel Canal+ was the first real pay-TV station to start operations. Later, Abril acquired half of Canal+ and launched its channel in a joint venture called TVA (Mageste, 1989). While Globo maintained complete secrecy about its plans, Fontoura divulged impressive projects for his channel that, likewise, was not on the air by the time of this study. The concessions for other parts of the country followed, as a general rule, affiliation to these pioneers. Pay television was not restricted to UHF channels, however. Soon afterwards, the government conceded SHF channels to Canal+, and Globo found a breach in the law to launch its satellite delivered channels. As the following recollections indicate, the elitism of pay television did not made the industry less attractive and competitive.

5.3.1 Canal+ - A troubled beginning

It does not exist anymore, but the story of Canal+ and its young entrepreneur André Dreifuss was still talked about in the early 90s. Back from the United States with a degree and experience in television, Dreifuss would have convinced his father-in-law to invest in his ideas for a Brazilian pay-television station. Fortunately, his father-in-law was Mathias Machline, owner of several electronic companies, including Sharp do Brasil. In fact, Dreifuss implemented (or tried to) on Canal+ most of the services that characterized paid television in the country by the 1990s, making it the first STV and later the first MMDS system created in Brazil. It all began on March 28, 1989, when UHF subscription channel 29 of São Paulo started transmitting the programming of American cable channel ESPN. The initial $ 8 million invested by Machline provided for 16 daily hours of transmission, soon increased to 19 hours (from 6 A.M. to 1A.M.) (Mageste, 1989), but the subscribers were yet to be conquered. The initial free preview period would indicate the difficulty of the task. After all, Dreifuss had to look for television viewers that had the necessary language skills to understand the English transmissions, an interest in such foreign sports as golf, a UHF reception capability and significant disposable cash. At the time of the premiere, a decoder cost NCz$150 and the monthly fee was a tenth of that (Magyar, 1989).

If the market penetration was hard and slow, however, the service and technology enhancements were fast and impressive. Fueled by increasing investments, Canal+ started broadcasting in stereo on August 26, 1989 in preparation for the future use of the SAP (Second Audio Channel) technology, which would allow for the transmission of dubbed audio on the second channel. The mild public response was only offset at the time by the resale of ESPN excerpts, whose exclusivity it held, to other VHF channels like Cultura, Gazeta and Globo (1989c). It was only on December 2, 1989 that Canal+ added commercials to its programming. The advertising content was mainly institutional or for highly priced products and took just eight minutes of every hour, even though the Brazilian legislation allowed for fifteen. Soon, spots from McDonald's, Sears, Volkswagen and Dillard's Department Store were responsible for about 20 percent of the profits (1990a). By the end of 1989, the improving situation already led Dreifuss to announce plans to open space for national independent productions and for the creation of a journalism crew (Mageste, 1989). While the full potential of the system had not yet been reached, the government was opening the concession of super high frequency channels and American cable networks were arriving in Brazil via new satellite systems.

The conditions were set for the establishment of MMDS systems in the country and, again, Dreifuss took the lead. On January 22, 1990, three new SHF channels—the Super Canal—were added. It was an $11 million investment ($6 million in equipment and $5 million in programming), with return expected in four or five years (Marsiaj, 1990a). SHF channel 5 of São Paulo retransmitted the American cable channel CNN 24 hours a day, holding an exclusive contract for Brazil. In May 1989, Renato Pachetti, president of RAI Corporation, an American subsidiary of the Italian state network, visited South America and was approached by Dreifuss, who was interested in the RAI programming. But the RAI retransmission rights almost did not come to Super Canal. RAI's Pachetti first asked for the approval of his personal friend Roberto Irineu Marinho, owner of Globo TV, who was known to be interested in a similar project (Gancia, 1990). RAI programming consisted of variety shows, including Italian music, concerts and ecology programs. The most important program was the news bulletin, broadcast live from Italy between 7 and 9 P.M. The rest of the 12 hours of transmissions was filled by repetitions of the news bulletin, shows, movies, soccer and even a culinary program.

The third channel, SHF 2, presented 24 hours of videoclips furnished by CBS, BMG, Ariola, EMI-Odeon, Stiletto and other recording companies. The so-called TVM channel also included videotext-like news from UPI (United Press International), all edited and generated from a studio at Avenida Paulista (Vizia, 1990). The name and programming were a poor mimic of American cable channel MTV (Music Television), whose $2 million programming Dreifuss could not afford to contract in an earlier offer (Netto, 1990). Such an odd programming package must have had an equally odd audience, but not much subscriber data was ever released by Canal+. The only survey mentioned by the press happened in 1990 and indicated that 68 percent of subscribers were men and 32 percent were women, primarily between 25 and 40 years old. It also revealed that 83 percent preferred the original sound track in English and 93 percent had traveled outside the country (Vizia, 1990). The expansion of the subscriber base would, nevertheless, require effort to make the programming more accessible and more attractive. In this manner, a second audio channel started to be used for Portuguese transmissions and, while all subscribers—even those without stereo TV sets—could have it at no extra cost, the company had to pay an estimated $48,000.

The first Portuguese transmission happened on February 3, 1990, when a Brazilian tennis player narrated the live transmission of a tennis match between Brazil and Canada for the Davis Cup in Toronto (1990b). Business seemed to be getting better by July, as Canal+ started operating in Rio de Janeiro with UHF channel 48. Other expansion plans of the time listed Porto Alegre and Curitiba in the south of Brazil, besides 12 other cities around the country, to be reached through franchised systems (Vizia, 1990). Dreifuss even had plans to create another channel dedicated only to movies all day long, but by the end of 1990, Showtime, the partnership of Dreifuss and Machline, had invested more than $10 million without finding the formula for success. Interferences, sudden cuts in the programming, lack of trained personnel to "install the UHF/SHF antennas in a VHF city," uninteresting programs, too much repetition of programs and all sorts of technical difficulties caused a bad picture on the subscribers' sets and on the company budget graphs (Vizia, 1990).

Some industry observers then declared the failure of pay-TV in the so-called "Globoland." That was certainly not the case, although changes were urged. In essence, even more investments were necessary while sales and promotional efforts had to match technical advances. Dreifuss' experiments may have set the tone for the industry, but they consumed huge investments without ever defining a marketing strategy. Thus, Mathias Machline, who was a major partner in the Canal+ and owner of 50 percent of Super Canal, started to look for a new partner with the financial and technical/marketing backup that the company needed. With 17,000 subscriptions in São Paulo and 5,000 in Rio de Janeiro, the Showtime experiment was cancelled in November 1990 when Dreifuss sold his shares to Machline, leaving the company (Comodo, 1991).

5.3.2 Yes, we *also* have TVA

In the same month that Dreifuss left, his shares were resold by Machline to a new partner—Abril, the same group that was successfully launching MTV in Brazil and that had recently won the concession for pay-TV channels in Rio de Janeiro and São Paulo (Comodo, 1991). The new joint-venture, called Delta Telecomunicações, was to have a renewed impulse with more investments and the characteristic Abril way of doing business—i.e. marketing oriented. Indeed, Delta consumed in that same year $20 million of the $50 million invested by Abril Group in 1990, when the raw profits were $810 million (Monteiro, 1991b). As it had happened on MTV, the young generation assumed command. Beside 25-year-old Paulo Machline, son of Mathias, was 27-year-old Giancarlo Civita, grandson of Victor Civita, the founder of Abril. Supported by an experienced staff and plentiful resources, their task was to transform Canal+ into TVA (the "A" may stand for "Assinatura" [or Subscription], or even Abril), reformulating the old service and incorporating Abril's UHF channel. It was a significant change that involved not only variations in the programming, but also in the technical operations and marketing strategies. The objectives were to put together a package that would attract more people, fix reception problems mainly associated with the receivers' antennas, make subscription easier and use Abril's respectable name as a good product warranty.

The incorporation of UHF channels 24 in São Paulo and 54 in Rio de Janeiro with an all-movies lineup was certainly the most important feature of the new TVA Brasil Radioenlaces Ltda (Abril's company in the Delta joint-venture). The Brazilian version of American movie channels like Cinemax and Showtime was simply called "TVA Filmes" and spared further surveys to prove that movies, especially those from Hollywood, remained one of the most in-demand products among all segments of the market. The movies came with five-year exclusivity contracts from large distributors like CBS-Fox, Columbia, TriStar, Universal, Paramount, Orion, Disney/Touchstone and also European distributors like French Gaumont, Beaumont and Lumière (Delmanto, 1991). Initially, TVA bought a package of 600 movies, 360 of them unseen before on Brazilian television, to fill 16 hours (noon to 4 A.M.) of daily programming. About eight movies—one of them previously unseen on television—were presented each day, with repetitions at different times on the following days (19910). In May 1992, the programming was expanded to 24 hours and 12 movies a day, with the promised inclusion of more movies from distributors like Playboy and Touchstone/Disney. In fact, these were companies Abril had known for years as publisher of the Brazilian issues of Playboy and Disney magazines, which justified announcements that besides programs like "Playboy Late Hours" and "Inside Out," TVA would soon add a sixth channel with Disney programming for children (Iori, 1992). TVA Filmes was also the window to a few locally produced— or just edited—segments, designed to attract new subscribers with unscrambled transmissions. A series of short programs showed the behind-the-scenes activities of. Hollywood productions ("Luzes, Câmera, Ação"), curiosities about the movie world ("Takes") and facts about what happened in Hollywood on the same date in the past ("Neste dia em Hollywood"). Special events, like cinema festivals, had been announced to be covered by free-lance news crews.

Behind and in front of the Brazilian cameras was Rubens Ewald Filho, one of the best known movie critics of the country. After years of writing for Abril's magazines, he became Program Director of TVA and host of two shows. On Saturday nights, at 8:30 P.M., he hosted "Premiere," with commentaries about movies at the theaters, new video releases and news about movies in production stage. At the same time, on Mondays, he presented a European movie on a program called "Espaço Belas Artes," result of an agreement with the theater chain of the same name (19910); to the frustration of non-subscribers, his presentation was not scrambled, but the movie (that follows it) was. The American sitcom "Married with Children" was the only program always open to the general public, on weekdays at 8 P.M., and always dubbed in Portuguese (Schwartsman, 1991b). In fact, as the leading channel of TVA, the movies received special attention with regard to the Portuguese adaptations. The oldest movies (80 percent) only got subtitles, the new movies were just dubbed (20 percent), and the big hits of all times had both dubbed versions and versions with subtitles. For the first time in Brazil, the subtitles were being edited through a computer process. The translator input the text right into the computer and marked the start and ending time on the screen. In this manner, a movie could be subtitled in one week—half of the normal time—by one person instead of three. Translation and orthography mistakes had been corrected by a group of four people; and they had been finding lots of them. In "Wall Street," for example, rare roast beef became "unusual roast beef." The correction is communicated to the distributors and new video copies are also corrected. Censorship was also found. When "Godfather" was translated, for example, it was prohibited to mention drug traffic in Brazil (19910).

The old Canal+ lineup was also reformulated to attract a broader variety of subscribers. First, TVM was extinguished as an unnecessary competitor to the real MTV owned by Abril. Then, the RAI channel became two daily hours of live evening transmission on the Supercanal channel, which offered a total of 12-18 hours of daily programming. The rest of Supercanal's schedule was filled with news from the three American networks: "Meet the Press" and "Nightly News" from NBC, "Good Morning America" and "World News Tonight" from ABC, and "This Morning" from CBS—besides a selection of programs from various American cable channels like The Discovery Channel, Fashion Channel, Travel Channel and videoclips from the American Top Ten (Rodrigues, 1991) (Comodo, 1991).

TVA still held the exclusive rights in Brazil for the integral transmission of ESPN and CNN programming, but they too had gone through changes. Since February 4, 1991, CNN International replaced the CNN program aimed at the American market, on the new TVA Noticias (Serapicos, 1991). To compete with GloboSat national programming, TVA promised the coverage of national sports by a well-known producer (whose name was not revealed) along with ESPN shows on the TVA Esportes channel (Moreira, 1992). Together with the scrambling of CNN signals on PanamSat satellite on January 28, 1991, the Turner Company also started transmitting the programming of its cable channel TNT to all of Latin America. Turner Filmes do Brasil, a local subsidiary in Rio de Janeiro, first planned to offer the programming to one of the upcoming cable systems, but soon negotiated an exclusive contract with TVA for its Latin transmissions. For TVA, it represented 3,700 movies, 1,150 short productions and 450 cartoons produced up to the 1970s, which were part of TNT's Metro Goldwin Meyer library. The schedule of TVA Clássicos consisted of five new movies (rerun on the same day) on weekdays, about eight on weekends and holidays; because of the size of the collections, the movies were likely to be repeated again only after four months. Giancarlo Civita indicated that the agreement with TNT was to dub the movies in Brazil, send them back to Atlanta, and receive the whole programming package through the satellite, making it the first TVA channel in Portuguese (besides TVA Filmes). But up to mid-1992, the TNT programming still had only the equally foreign Spanish subtitles added to the original sound track (Schwartsman, 1991a).

Enhanced programming would not be enough, anyway, to escape the same fate as Canal+. TVA signals had to arrive at subscribers' TV sets with a more reasonable quality, and previous experience indicated that most receiver antennas were not adequate to tune higher frequencies. TVA had to invest about $2 million to change obsolete antennas in many buildings (Iori, 1992). The approximately 200 technicians, recruited among electric engineering students and community antenna repairmen, would go to the residences and measure the strength of the signals, recommending solutions that usually involve the installation of higher towers or more appropriate antennas. In case the quality of the image received was not satisfactory due to geographical problems (buildings or trees between the residence antenna and the transmitter can affect the reception of SHF signals) or poor residential installations, the technicians could recommend that the potential viewer not purchase the service. Another $15-20 million were spent on new equipment. In this manner, TVA was trying to avoid the criticism of bad signal reception that undermined the Canal+ operations. The improvement on customer service, though, was miscalculated. The initial flow of orders was so great that many subscribers complained about waits of 20 to 30 days before the visit of a technician (Iori, 1992). Another technical issue feared by TVA officials was the choice of decoder and pirating protection level. For reasons that may have ranged from the inventive Brazilian character to the widespread pirate wave that plagued the last days of American STV, TVA was said to have taken extreme measures against piracy. A source that preferred to remain anonymous commented that the initial grade of security adopted was too high (the range is 1-13) and even the subscribers could not quite capture the signals. New chips were needed in each decoder and American consultants had to coordinate the exchange process, during which no subscription was charged and no new ones were sold. Later on, the grade two level that was adopted still makes piracy difficult, but the subscribers seem to be free of problems.

According to this same source, this was just one of a series of stories of the early days of TVA, involving bad management, misuse of the company funds and corruption. The choice of decoder was no less awkward, even though TVA led an industry agreement for the adoption of a common model, which would allow the use of one unique decoder by subscribers of multiple companies. After prolonged studies, as described in the previous chapter, the option for General Electric's TOCOM meant the early retirement and substitution of each one of the thousands of Zenith decoders used by Canal+, while an oversized order of about 200,000 new sets was said to have been bought. And these numbers also included remote controls, which TVA provided free of charge, unlike most American cable systems at the time, which rented them to customers. There were, indeed, many problems to be solved before the company could really start operations. Among these initial difficulties that TVA had to face was a legal suit brought by the French channel Plus (+) regarding the unauthorized use of the name and the logotype by Canal+ (1991i). Moreover, this anonymous source mentioned that the company almost went bankrupt at one point, due to the purchase of a huge fleet of cars for technicians, together with gas stations and repair shops, which raised the company's fixed assets to unbearable levels. Fortunately, most of these problems never reached the subscribers—or the press—leaving TVA the chance of restructuring itself with new staff members and the importation of Abril's aggressive marketing.

On May 1991, the sale of subscriptions was suspended while the product was redefined and a more efficient sales and installation structure was put in place. Three packages were offered to the subscribers: the UHF system, with TVA Filmes (movies) and TVA Esportes (ESPN); the SHF system, with TVA Notícias (CNN), TVA Supercanal (news potpourri) and TVA Clássicos (TNT); and a complete package, with both systems (Comodo, 1991). The approximately 25,000 subscribers of Canal+ did not pay the installation fees and received a 30 percent discount on their renewals, while new subscribers were attracted by a $1.5 million launching campaign in São Paulo (Anderaos, 1991b). Among other promotions, a colorful program guide was distributed to various restaurants, a luxurious showroom was set up in the richest neighborhood of São Paulo, and some of Sharp's point-of-sales also helped sell subscriptions. The target was to have 30,000 subscriptions by the end of September 1991, 45,000 by the end of the year and one million within five years (Schwartsman, 1991b). On July 24, 1991, the sale of new subscriptions restarted with rather unique financing characteristics. While a house resident could pay something between $500 and almost $3,000 in January 1992 (See Table 8), different options were offered to apartment residents, who were led into convincing their neighbors to subscribe so that they all could enjoy significant installation discounts. If three to six apartments subscribed within the same building, their discount on the installation fee was ten percent,

Table 8 - Prices of TVA packages

	UHF	SHF	UHF+SHF
Installation	1,826	1,508	2,535
Subscription + Decoder			
House	508	842	906
Building			
Individual*	2,223	1,906	2,732
All Apartments	2,271	3,630	4,797

* The subscription and installation costs are shared by building residents. Values are equivalent to dollars in January 1992.

Source: TVA Showroom salespeople. São Paulo, January 1992.

for instance. Between seven and ten, the discount was 20 percent; between 11 and 60 it was 50 percent, and for more than that it was free. If new subscribers were later added in the same building, the others were reimbursed and the new ones paid only for the initial subscription (which included the price of the decoder). Contrary to Canal+ marketing, TVA did not offer collective decoders in buildings; each subscriber had his own decoder (19910). The monthly rates varied around $30 or, in the case of UHF package, just enough to rent at least ten videotapes in a large rental store (1991y). The "salty" prices, however, did not seem to diminish the public interest for TVA, as demonstrated by the initial results of the free preview.

On June 9, 1991, TVA started experimental broadcasting and a free preview followed, which mixed on UHF channels 24 and 29 the programming of all TVA's five channels for 12 to 14 hours daily (6 to 12 A.M.). In the first day of free preview, TVA received 800 calls, which led to 300 subscription reservations by the end of the week (19910). The five-channel package was the most popular one sold in TVA's first weeks, corresponding to 52 percent of sales. The UHF option had 40 percent of sales and the SHF option only eight percent (1991y). The relatively low demand for the SHF option can be explained by the transmission difficulties described in the previous chapter, the language barriers (since the programming was in English, Spanish or Italian) and, to an extent yet to be calculated, the poor appeal of the programming. In regard to this latter possibility, a saleswoman at the TVA showroom commented that the company had been installing the CNN channel alone in some flat-service apartment hotel condominiums, which usually house foreign executives temporarily doing business in São Paulo. She also added that multinational companies have developed the habit of transferring subscriptions among foreign employees coming to and going from Brazil (1992). The positive results of this free trial period resulted in, among other reasons, a delayed official start, from the forecast date of September 1 to the 15, 1991, when the signals were scrambled at exactly 12 P.M. By that time, the payoff was expected to come 70 percent from sales of subscriptions and 30 percent from sales of advertising space (Americana, 1991). With different advertising policies for each channel, by August TVA had already conquered advertisers like General Motors and Brahma (beverages), besides the in-house ads of Sharp (Santomauro, 1991). Until mid-1992, the very rare commercials that could be seen were in between the movies shown on TVA Filmes. The expectation was that these numbers would grow with the expansion of the system to the rest of the country. The area covered by TVA corresponded more or less to the inner borders of metro São Paulo, but it already had the right to transmit to another 16 cities. In Rio de Janeiro (UHF channels 48 and 58) and Curitiba, where Canal+ used to operate, too, experimental broadcasting started in March 1992 and it was planned that scrambling would begin in April (Moreira, 1992).

According to Program Director Giancarlo Civita, the next cities to be reached were Porto Alegre (Rio Grande do Sul South), Brasília (Federal District) and Belo Horizonte (Minas Gerais - Central West). The affiliates or branches in these cities would receive the NTSC stereo signals via satellite, but the Pal-M standard was used to broadcast locally. Except for TVA Filmes and TVA Supercanal, which were edited in São Paulo and retransmitted through two full transponders of Brasilsat, all the imported signals were captured directly from PanamSat. By May 1992, the balance of operations for TVA and its approximately 750 employees (including 200 technicians, 200 administrative workers and 100 program producers) were fairly good, considering the great economic crisis impoverishing the country. Even though investments had reached $30 million and TVA was said to be spending even more on the purchase of three half-transponders at Brasilsat II, about 34,200 subscribers were conquered and the forecasts were bright. By the end of the year, TVA expected to have 100,000 subscribers in São Paulo, 30,000 in Rio de Janeiro and 10,000 in Curitiba. That is, if the recession did not get worse. In that case, the target numbers would have to be reduced by 30 percent (Moreira, 1992).

5.3.3 GloboSat - Competition comes from the sky

On the same day that TVA started its experimental broadcasting, Globo TV transmitted announcements throughout the whole day asking people not to subscribe to any pay television system before getting to know GloboSat's services. The advertising piece was called "Don't subscribe to anything without seeing it" (Delmanto, 1991) and, while it was a clear show of force to slow the competitor's growth, it was also a sign of the Globo Group's indecision regarding pay television. Like·Abril, in 1988 Globo had received concessions for UHF pay channels in Rio de Janeiro and São Paulo, but by mid-1992 had not presented any sign of an opening date. On the contrary, director Antonio Athayde of TV Paulista Metro, channel 19 of São Paulo, maintained total secrecy about the station's plans (Fernandes, 1990). Surprisingly, the actions of Globo favored instead the launching of the DBS-like services of GloboSat, which were not even anticipated by the legislation of 1988. GloboSat was not formally allowed to operate or sell subscriptions in August 1991, but GloboSat's competitive efforts did not wait for any approval to start distributing flyers and brochures about its system to condominiums and houses in Rio and São Paulo (Delmanto, 1991). In fact, the decision to anticipate such promotions from September to August was based on some previous legislative changes that finally cleared the way for the new service. The National Secretary of Communications confirmed that GloboSat provided a service that did not require government authorization. A presidential decree of July 18, 1991 ruled on the so-called "special services of satellite communication" including the transmission of data, television and certain telephone signals—but there were still no specific norms for each service. Since the norms were what were legally needed to define how the applicant should proceed, GloboSat did not have to apply for any authorization. According to the legislation of the time (dating back to 1962) regarding the use of satellite transponders, the renters were free to use them as they wanted, without any interference from the government (1991q).

GloboSat used regular low-powered C-Band satellite transponders to deliver four channels to parabolic antenna owners within the Brasilsat II satellite footprint. In spite of the delay in comparison to TVA, the system was under implementation for quite a while. Newspaper articles report that the president of Globo Group, Roberto Marinho, provided the capital and also rented four transponders long before the company was formed, paying $400,000 per month for them. In this manner, he not only secured the existence of his future service, but precluded any prospective competitors from starting operations before at least two years, when the new Brazilian satellite was scheduled to be launched (Apolinário, 1991). The other equal partners of Horizonte Comunicações, the managing company created in 1982, were José Bonifácio de Oliveira Sobrinho (known as "Boni")—vice-president of Globo TV for 24 years—and Joseph Wallach (Delmanto, 1991). Wallach was the representative from American Time-Life that, in 1966, lent $3 million to Globo newspaper to create its television network. Naturalized as a Brazilian citizen, for 15 years he was the Financial and Administrative Vice-President of Globo. In 1981 Wallach left Globo and returned to America, but Marinho was said to have called him back, waving GloboSat as a gift (Serapicos & Sastre, 1991). The news of that time highlighted the huge initial investments of Marinho in his effort to bring Wallach to the company, while he was involved in some other successful enterprises. In 1985, Wallach organized Telemundo in San Diego, a Spanish language network, with broadcasting in ·Miami, New York, Los Angeles, San Francisco, Chicago, Houston and Puerto Rico (Apolinário,1991).

It was not a surprise, therefore, that many credited Wallach for the aggressive marketing that characterized GloboSat from the beginning, while Boni and Marinho remained distant from the company operations. Wallach's teaser spot, aimed at reducing the impact of TVA's free preview, also attracted subscribers to GloboSat, which started reserving subscriptions on July 1, 1991—even before an actual programming package could be made available. Thus, when the experimental broadcasting started, at noon of October 26, 1991, the public interest was already high. In the first three weeks of subscription sale in November, about 10,000 new viewers were quickly added (Moreira, 1992). The target for GloboSat was to sell 70,000 subscriptions in the first year and 500,000 within four years (Silva, 1991). Considering the elitism of the system and industry estimates that there were only 160,000 parabolic antennas installed in the whole country (in 1992), these seemed very optimistic goals. The sales manager for São Paulo, Renata Silva, agreed that most subscribers were from class AA, living in the rich condominiums of selected neighborhoods (See Table 9), but indicated that GloboSat intended to serve most of Latin America and that it had been installing new antennas at discount rates for many subscribers (Silva, 1992). In fact, what had restricted the company's operations to a few cities in the Southern cone of Brazil was only the capacity of selling, installing and maintaining the equipment necessary to receive and decode the satellite signals—a 3.6 meter parabolic antenna, a decoder, a modulator for each channel and coaxial cables. The approximately 900 people (150 technicians and 150 administrators in São Paulo, plus 600 others in Rio de Janeiro) who composed the initial staff of the company had quickly become insufficient to service the increasing demand that included, for example, rich farmers in the Central West region, who were not reached by the signals of any regular station (Silva, 1992).

Table 9 - GloboSat subscriptions

Per city
70% São Paulo
30% Rio de Janeiro and Southern region
Per residency
50% Condominiums
40% Residence Hotels
10% Houses

Source: Estimates provided by São Paulo Sales Manager, Renato Silva, interviewed on January 22, 1992.

165

Renata Silva explained that a group of fifteen American technicians from various equipment providers participated in the creation of the company as consultants. Besides its own maintenance crew, twelve other companies were recruited as representatives. The plans for 1992 included the opening of an office in the state of Minas Gerais and many cooperative contracts with Globo TV affiliates, which would handle sales and installation in other regions of the country. In the war for subscribers, the press repeatedly compared GloboSat and TVA, but the conclusion was always left to the two percent of the population that Wallach recognized as targets (Sastre, 1991). The most common criticism of GloboSat was related to its commercialization. While TVA sold both individual and/or collective subscriptions in buildings, with their simpler receivers and compact decoders, GloboSat only sold the latter kind. Manager Silva confirmed that the subscriptions to buildings used to require an absolute majority (every resident would have to agree to subscribe), but there were plans to sell subscriptions in cases where at least 50 percent of the residents signed up. The reason was simple; the installation of a rather big parabolic antenna on the top of a building demanded the approval of all residents, who will have to bear the extra municipal taxes associated with it. The tiering was also different. All of GloboSat's four channels were present in its five different packages, distinguished only by the number of outlets installed (See Table 10), instead of by channels offered, like TVA. The range of installation prices varied from $3,000 for a single outlet to $7,000 for multiple outlets, allowing many TV sets to simultaneously tune different channels. A TV guide (much less fancy than TVA's), remote control and maintenance services were included in the monthly fee, which ranged $35-20, depending upon the number of subscribers in the system.

Thus, in many cases, price differentiation strategies did not apply to this war. Even though estimates were published that GloboSat would cost five times more than the other subscription systems through UHF and SHF (Apolinário, 1991), the satellite system could be advantageous, especially in some buildings. The second most controversial issue in the Brazilian pay television war was the quality of the signals delivered to subscribers. TVA's use of higher frequencies (UHF/SHF) was accused of suffering heavy interference from obstacles in the cities. While GloboSat's transmissions used

Table 10 - GloboSat's Tiering

Kit	Number of Outlets	Price (dollars)
1	1	
2	2	
3	3	3,000 to 7,000
4	4	
5	multiple*	

* Each TV set has its own decoder, allowing different channels to be watched simultaneously.

Source: Personal Interview with GloboSat São Paulo Sales Manager Renata A. V. Silva on January 22, 1992.

even higher frequencies (K band), they were supposed to be clearer, as they came directly from the sky, with fewer plausible obstacles (Cappia, 1992). On the other hand, GloboSat was accused of using half of a transponder for each channel, which implied the need for more powerful receiver antennas. As mentioned before, Horizonte Comunicações had four transponders at Brasilsat II, used in the following manner: one full transponder for its news channel, one transponder and a half for the other three channels, and one full transponder and a half vacant. The company's abundance was justified by plans of a future fifth channel and safety procedures; that is, in case one transponder fails another one can substitute for it. Nevertheless, most of the press recognized it as a monopolistic action to avoid competition (Andrade, 1991; Apolinário, 1991). The GloboSat advantage was based on the use of satellites, vital tools for every modern communication system of broad range, and on the presentation of a good programming lineup. In essence, it looked exactly like TVA's, with a channel for sports, another for movies, news and shows. But the two decades of know-how that TV Globo had accumulated certainly contributed to a more national accent. Unlike TVA, which purchased a complete programming package that was ready to transmit, the GloboSat programming was defined by the company, which purchased programs one by one from a variety of producers and syndicators. The purchase decisions at GloboSat were made by Brazilian professionals, who promised to offer variety of

167

programming, so that the best events were never transmitted at the same time (Andrade, 1991).

This local character was stated from the beginning, with a policy to fill at least 25 percent of the transmissions with national shows and events (Carvalho, 1991). The foreign programs had also been converted to Portuguese, and the company estimated that 90 percent of them were either dubbed or subtitled. From a studio built in Rio de Janeiro, where all the shows were put together, the signals were uplinked through its own ground station and, even though they were not in stereo, there was a potential for it in the future. The news channel was called GNT (GloboSat Notícias) and transmitted 16 hours of news from a variety of sources, like Visinews, TWTN, BBC (London), Eurovision, the three American networks and even CNN. Some of the latest advertising for GloboSat emphasized the offer of CNN bulletins, on which TVA held a monopoly for integral (24-hour) transmission, but not for the simple use of images or short news casts, as most television networks in Brazil do. Every morning it presented a financial program with the indexes in the major international stock markets (1991g). Brazilian professionals anchored the bulletins, and each full hour was scheduled to have a five minute bulletin with national and international news produced by Globo TV crews. Paulo Francis, a well-known Globo TV correspondent based in New York, was also scheduled to have a program interviewing some international personalities. The sports channel transmitted 16 hours a day, and besides soccer, the national game, many international competitions were covered through contracts with several sources, including ESPN. GloboSat's research, however, indicated that the Brazilian elite appreciated only a handful of ESPN shows and concentrated on tennis, water and winter sports. Instead of hosts, the Top Sport channel used animated vignettes and narration off camera (Rita, 1991a).

Telecine was the 24-hour movie channel and, like TVA, GloboSat negotiated contracts in 1991 with several large American distributors, such as Columbia, Warner, Paramount, and Metro Goldwin Meyer. Independents like Orion, Savern, and New World, besides 150 Brazilian productions, were also scheduled (Rito, 1991a). In order to fill 12 sessions a day (every other hour a new movie), GloboSat was counting on Globo TV's library of 10, 000 movies, for which permanent rights had already been purchased. Since the company was not selling advertising space in this first phase, the intervals were filled with interviews, curiosities and news from an exclusive correspondent in Hollywood (Silva, 1992). The 18 hours of variety shows on the MultiShow channel included programming for the Japanese, German and French colonies in Brazil. The programs from ZDF (Germany), NHK, (Japan) and Anthene 2 (France) were presented with the original soundtracks and subtitles (Rito, 1991a). Old European movies and "cult" cartoons, like "The Simpsons" and "The Adams Family" were also scheduled, but the constant variation of programs on this channel indicated its tendency to be the laboratory for GloboSat productions and special imports (Rito, 1991b). For example, the Venezuelan soap opera "Cristal," one of the highest successes in the Latin American market, was bought by Globo Films in December 1990 and was presented by GloboSat (Rita, 1991b). With 200 chapters, it was aired daily between 7 and 8 P.M., not competing with the Globo TV primetime soaps. The producers of "Telecurso," a secondary educational program transmitted by Globo TV very early in the morning, were scheduled to produce a similar program, dealing with subjects of interest to the elite subscribers, like how to ride a jet ski (Sastre, 1991). By May 1992, such programming, supported by an investment of $40 million, had conquered about 16,000 subscribers—and the competition is just starting (Iori, 1992).

5.3.4 PluralSat - Television's European accent

Since December 1991, GloboSat had not been alone in the Brazilian skies. Through transponder 11 of Brasilsat II, PluralSat programming was offered 12 hours a day to anyone interested in German and French affairs. The lineup consisted of shows, movies and documentaries of German channels ZDF and ARD, besides French channels Antenne 2, FR3, TF1, Canal+, La Cinq and M6. The signals were not scrambled until March 1992, but superintendent Márcio Rebello stated prices were $70 semi-annually for houses and $860 for buildings (Moreira, 1992). More information about PluralSat was not available during this study, but its focus on the German and French colonies in Brazil

169

hardly represented strong competition for the other systems.

5.3.5 TV Alpha - Bring me your elite...

The association of brothers Lauro, director of Bandeirantes TV (1991n), and Walter Fontoura, director of the O Globo newspaper, in the Pira Som & Imagem company conquered the concession of UHF channel 50 of São Paulo in 1988. But Walter quickly sold his share of the enterprise to his brother, who had been struggling ever since to launch the pay-service TV Alpha. Lauro Fontoura initially invested $3.2 million and planned to be the first to start operations in November 1989. The programming plans were to stay on the air 20 to 24 hours a day, transmitting subtitled original versions of foreign channels in stereo for a class A public, between 35 and 40 years old (Mageste, 1989). In the beginning of 1990, however, Lauro announced new plans: Alpha was scheduled to start experimental broadcasting in May and subscription sales in July. At that point, he had already spent $1. 2 million on equipment, like a sophisticated Rhode Schwartz transmitter, and had $750,000 available in liquid capital, plus $500,000 for a launching campaign. His idea was to start with ten hours on air, adding blocks of four hours in the following phases.

The programming would basically come from BBC Europe—a bundle of English channels that BBC 1 and BBC 2 sold to twelve other European countries—and would gradually increase from eight hours daily to a maximum of 18 hours, representing 75 percent of the schedule (Marsiaj, 1990b). The contract with BBC would involve concerts, ballets and other shows, besides two important news bulletins to be broadcast simultaneously with London at 5 and 9 P.M. (London time) (Pimenta, 1990). The 25 percent of the programming generated in Brazil would be composed of a guide to services (especially leisure) in São Paulo, and foreign movies like "Quo Vadis" and "A vida de Verdi," which had already been purchased (Pimenta, 1990) (Marsiaj, 1990b). The insertion of commercials was limited to four intervals of two minutes for each hour of programming, and Lauro promised the introduction of the brand-exclusivity concept in Brazil. In practical terms, it meant that Alpha would only advertise one brand of each product (Pimenta, 1990).The monthly fee was estimated in NCz$18, taking advantage of the apparent boost of the economy caused by the last government changes in the economy. The expectation was to have between 25,000 and 50,000 subscribers in one year (Fernandes, 1990), and about 82 employees worked hard in the 450-square-meter studio to start operations in 1990 (Pimenta, 1990).

Lauro had joined Abril in the choice of a common decoder brand, General Electric's TOCOM, and the Bogner antenna was provisionally located in the corner of Avenida Paulista and Rua da Consolação, with transmission power of 316 kW (Picillo, 1989). The decline of the economy by late 1990, however, deeply affected TV Alpha's plans. In 1991, Lauro announced that he had invested $800,000 to set up the station and $2 million more were needed to close the contract with BBC. Since then, very little news had been published about TV Alpha, and its future was still unclear. By the time of this study, Lauro Fontoura was said to be signing a contract with Bandeirantes TV for an operational agreement that would let him use the network's installations, engineering facilities and even the programming (1991b). Aiming at the *creme* de la *crème,* the elite of the elite, the TV Alpha project may have lacked the necessary public and financial support to realize better prospects.

6
Audience Segmentation

... since so little of your message is going to get through anyway, you ignore the sending side and concentrate on the receiving end. You concentrate on the perceptions of the prospect. Not the reality of the product (Ries & Trout, 1981, p.9).

At the heart of market segmentation is the concept that viewers/consumers are too complex and differentiated to be treated as a single mass while, at the same time, homogeneous enough to be classified into small groups. The trick seems to be identifying the variable (or combination of variables) that characterizes a specific group and differentiates it from others. Kotler arranges such variables in four large categories: geographic (region, city, density, climate), demographic (age, sex, family size, family life cycle, income, occupation, education, religion, race, nationality), psychographic (social class, life style , personality) and behaviorist (purchase occasion, benefits sought, user status, usage rate, loyalty status, readiness stage, attitude toward product) (Kotler, 1986).

The television segmentation promoted by the cable networks in the United States segmented viewer groups using a combination of demographic and behaviorist variables (See Table 1). Since the network's coverage is national and psychographics were more or less implicit in the demographic variables, these categories have apparently not significantly influenced the American segmentation process. In the American situation, explains Ien Ang, the audience is defined by two features: size (number of viewers at a certain time) and composition (demographics). In "Desperately Seeking the Audience," Ang relates the development of the American rating system and the segmentation process:

> The growing emphasis on demographic information ...was a direct consequence of the advertisers' wish to advertise their products to

Table 1 - American cable networks per variable

Network	Category	Variable
ESPN	Behaviouristic	Enthusiastic attitude toward sports
CNN	Behaviouristic	Benefit of news sought
Nickelodeon	Demographic	Age group
MTV	Behaviouristic Demographic	Enthusiastic attitude toward music (12-34 age)
Nashville	Behaviouristic	Enthusiastic attitude toward country music
Discovery	Behaviouristic	Education as benefit
Lifetime	Demographic	Women group
Weather Channel	Behaviouristic	Weather as benefit
Headline News	Behaviouristic	Benefit of news sought
A&E	Behaviouristic	Enthusiastic about arts
VH-1	Behaviouristic Demographic	Enthusiastic attitude toward music (25-45 age)
Financial News	Behaviouristic	Economy news as benefit
Black Entertainment	Demographic	Race group
Learning Channel	Behaviouristic	Education as benefit
Travel Channel	Behaviouristic	Travel information as benefit sought
Consumer News	Behaviouristic	Shopping news as benefit
Sports America	Behaviouristic	Enthusiastic attitude toward sports
Nostalgia	Demographic	Over 45 year old group
Comedy Channel	Behaviouristic	Comedy as benefit sought
Galavision	Demographic	Nationality, language

Source: Constructed by the author, based on Kotler's definitions in Kotler, P. Principles of Marketing. (3rd.Ed.) Englewood Cliffs, Prentice-Hall, 1986.

specific market segments - a development which has had a major impact on American network television since the late. 1960s... Through demographics the television audience is streamlined by neatly slicing it up in substantive segments, each of which consists of presumably well-organized, serialized viewers displaying dependable viewing behavior. Sometimes, typical characteristics are assigned to each segment which conjures up nicely contained subjectivities, formalized in so-called psychographics (Ang, 1992, p.63).

The patterns provided by the demographic-psychographics cross-data analysis enable broadcasters and advertisers to "develop simple practical truths," about the viewing and consumption behavior/ preferences of each niche of television audiences. But as demographic numbers change, the "truths" should be expected to change, too. In this sense, the numbers in the United States suggest very different conclusions than the Brazilian numbers (See Table 2). By the time of this study in the 1990s, America's population was almost twice that of Brazil. It was older, more educated and very much richer. The economy was more stable in America, with lower inflation and a more even distribution of wealth, which meant a larger consumer market and justified the expanded communication base.

Moreover, many variables in the Brazilian market were dichotomized. Instead of a large middle class, as in America, there was a small rich group, a small middle class, and a large portion of poor people in Brazil. The regions of the country were also more diverse. While the South and Southeast regions had stronger European influence and a very industrialized economy, the North and Northeast were particularly influenced by African cultures and had economies based on agriculture. Naturally, the first regions—especially the São Paula-Rio de Janeiro axis—were richer than the others and concentrated most of the population (See Figure 1), communication industries and advertisers.

Remarkably, eight percent of the Brazilian population alone accounted for 62 percent of the national consumption of goods and services, while 65 percent of workers made less than $650 per month. In "High Tech Alienation in Brazil," Omar S. Oliveira cites[9]:

> Between 1960 and 1980, the wealthiest ten percent of Brazilian society increased their earnings from 39.6 percent to 50.9 percent of the total, while the poorest half saw their participation slashed from 17.4 to 12.6 percent...The majority of Brazilians live under precarious conditions. For example, more than half of all homes

9 When compared to other sources, Oliveira's numbers seemed rather questionable and should be cautiously considered.

Table 2 - Selected Statistics

	United States	Brazil
Area	9,372,614 km2	8,511,965 km2
Population	246,113,000 (88)	147,404,375 (89)
Language	English	Portuguese
Religion		
Protestants	53%	
Catholics	40%	93%
Jewish	4%	
Ethnicity		
White/ Hispanics	83%	54.77%
Black	11.78%	5.89%
Asiatic	1.57%	
Native	0.6%	
Mulatos		38.45%
Pop. growth	0.9%	2.48% (70-80)
Pop distribution	73.9% urban (85)	76.2% urban (90)
Pop density	26.2 hab./ km2	17 hab./ km2
Age		
0-14	21.5%	41.5%
15-59	61.8%	57%
60+	16.7% (87)	6.68% (85)
Income per capita	$18,430 (87)	2,437 (88)
Social class		
A	6%	
B	20%	
C	30% (92)	
Gross National Product (GNP)	$4,486 trillion (87)	$351.9 billion (88)
GNP Growth	3.8% (88)	0.3% (88)
GNP percentages from		
Industry	18.9%	26.5%
Services	17.6%	13.2%
Commerce		13.8%
Agriculture	2.1% (87)	9.3% (86)

	United States	Brazil
Inflation	3.7% (87)	933.62% (88)
Labor		
Industry	15.7%	27.6%
Commerce	20%	26.3%
Services	19.9%	28%
Public Services		46.9% (85)
Female workers	44.3% of total	33.5% (85)
Unemployment	6.2% (87)	3.9% (89)
External debt	$368.2 billion (87)	$100.4 billion (89)
Birth rate (per 100 hab)	153 (88)	286 (85-89)
Mortalilty (per 100 hab)	94 (88)	79 (85-90)
Life expectancy (years)		
Men	72	62.3
Women	78.9	67.6 (85-90)
Child mortality (per 100 birth)	102 (87)	632 (85-90)
Illiteracy	4.5% (80)	17.6% (88)
Telephones	122,203,000 (86) susbcribers	7,892,387 (87) terminals
Newspapers Per 1000 hab	1,646 daily	279 daily
	266 issues (87)	62 issues (86)

Source: Almanaque Abril 1990. São Paulo, Editora Abril, 1990.

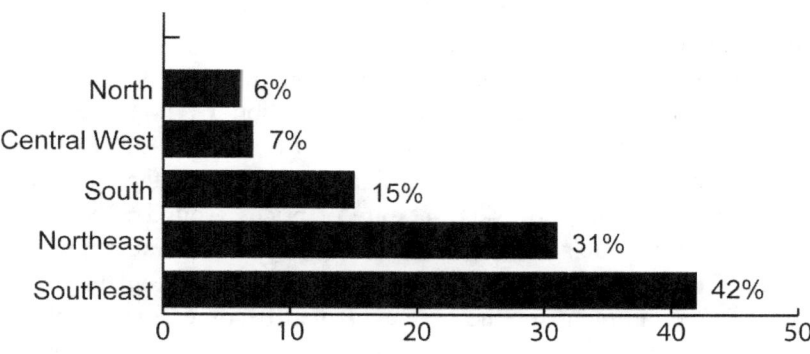

Figure 1 - Population of Brazilian regions in 1990.

Source: Anuário Estatístico do Brasil - 1989/90.

have no electricity, 79 percent no refrigerators, 71 percent no running water, 85 percent no sewage, and 60 percent of the population is either illiterate or semi-illiterate (Oliveira, 1992, p.8).

Such disparities within the Brazilian market were reflected in an apparent tendency to use social class rather than taste or psychographics in the television segmentation process (Bourdieu, 1984). The use of social class has been generally criticized for either being too narrow (Almeida & Wickerhauser, 1991) or not very useful in segmentation (Kamakura & Mazzoo, 1991). Researchers in the United States and Brazil have worked hard to develop a classification scheme to further segment the target market, known as the AIO (Activities, Interests and Opinions) or VALS Framework (Values and Lifestyles). Nonetheless, Brazilian broadcasters have traditionally defined the audience in terms of social class, and much of the theoretical research and associated literature on program choices of TV audiences employ the concept to date. Indeed, the third table in chapter three indicated how the use of the media can be inferred by social class. Reading materials and FM radio stations seem to be used more by the higher classes, while AM radio talk shows are preferred by lower classes. Television network SBT is the second option of the lower classes (after Globo), and Manchete the alternative at the time for the higher classes. Overall, however, television remains the most pervasive medium in Brazil, appreciated by all classes.

Thus, even though the product (audience) delivered by Brazilian television to advertisers presents significant disparities from the American one, calling for different segmentation categories— psychographics instead of behavioristics—both systems reach the majority of the population. Brazil had 28 million TV households in 1991 compared to 92 million of the United States (1991g) (Yuster, 1992). According to Oliveira, more than 73 percent of the Brazilian households had television sets, in spite of prices around $300 for a small color set, which were much beyond the typical worker's buying power (Oliveira, 1992). In fact, television had long been the main form of entertainment for the masses. It had become commonplace to indicate that women, children—and lower classes—were heavier viewers (See Figure 2), but television was still the cheapest leisure option for these demographic groups.

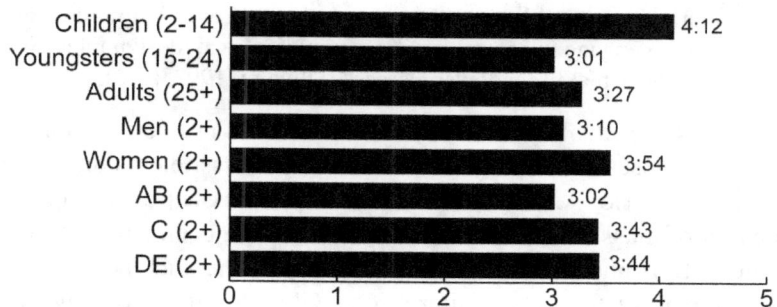

Figure 2 - Brazilian TV consumption per demographic groups.

Source: IBOPE (Instituto Brasileiro de Opinião Pública e Estatística), AIP Base - SP/RJ, 1990.

Hoineff explains that "thanks to a permanent social crisis that keeps the population at home, the television daily absorbs eight hours of the children's time and almost all of the leisure time of the adults" (Hoineff, 1991). Even without buying power to consume the products and services advertised on television, the lower classes constitute an important audience. In "A questão do público de TV no Brasil: reflexões sobre a pesquisa Lintas" Bolano cited in 1987 a survey conducted by the Brazilian research company Marplan in eight of the largest national markets, which concluded that up to 88 percent of the households of social class D and E have TV sets, while the percentage grows to 90 percent in class C[10].

"This happens in a country where classes A and B (less than 25 percent of the population) are responsible for more than 88 percent of the consumption," he explains (Bolano, 1988). Oliveira presents some more recent numbers and raises a question:

> Only ten percent of the Brazilian workforce makes more than $200 a month, and a mere one and a half percent above $600. The

10   The so-called ABA/ABIPEME (Associação Brasileira de Anunciantes/ Associação Brasileira de Pesquisadores de Mercado) criteria divides classes from A to E according to the number of points individuals sum for the predetermined social value of income and education, besides the ownership of several household utensils.

marketing contradiction becomes obvious: If only ten percent are able to engage in some sort of consumption, why design television schedules that fit the lower classes? (Oliveira, 1992, p.10).

Besides the ideological answers discussed in previous chapters, Oliveira proposes some pragmatic reasons for mass television in the Brazilian scenario. After all, "they [the lower classes] do engage in some sort of mass consumption (soap, soft drinks, beer, small radios, watches, etc.)" and compose the larger share of the audience, whose total numbers dictate advertising prices. Globo's rates, he suggests, were "among the highest in the world, an average of $500 per second because it has consistently held more than 80 percent[11] of the audience during primetime" (Oliveira, 1992). The total audience is still the main element that indicates the competitive position of the TV networks, but it has become increasingly more difficult to explain why car makers, for example, should advertise their $30,000 cars for TV viewers with the low purchasing qualifications just described. Illustrative was the example of the SBT network, which held the second-largest audience share in the country with a very lower, lower-middle class lineup. In spite of its positive ratings numbers, SBT did not make significant profits in its early days because the profile of its audience did not attract the higher quality advertisers. SBT had to convince them that its public did consume their goods/services before it could start drawing their advertising.

The value of a higher qualified audience, on the other hand, also remains undetermined. TV Manchete, which claimed an upper-class audience, had the lowest revenues of all networks (See Table 3) and an outstanding debt around $50 million. In 1990, it made $100 million and spent almost the same amount without a program hit above the ten percent audience share (1991p). While the misfortune of Manchete could also be explained by simple bad management, it constituted evidence that simply abandoning the secure ratings system for the lure of a "better" (more qualified) audience may not always be the smartest strategy. The inclusion of the large lower classes in the ratings may preclude those ratings from reflecting advertising effectiveness; and the quality of the audience does not always determine television

11   In fact, the audience ratings for TV Globo's primetime average between 40 and 50 percent.

profitability. Nevertheless, high ratings and upper-class audiences remain the name of the game. In the analysis of Ang, "as long as the map works, the industry will not bother to look for more 'realistic' maps." In other words: ... the concrete practices and experiences of actual audiences are irrelevant for the industry so long as the information delivered by audience measurement is uncontested and perceived to be adequate. Therefore, the gap will only be problematized when the streamlining process tends to slacken (Ang, 1992, p.67).

Table 3 - Brazilian networks' revenues - 1989

Network	Revenues (in millions)
Globo	596
SBT	152
Bandeirantes	78
Manchete	50

Source: "Os amigos na TV". São Paulo, Veja, June 26, 1991.

Evidence of that widening of the gap between audience measures and real individuals was given by the Brazilian survey agencies' disagreement about the size of the upper classes. In 1992, the institutes LPM/Burke and Marplan rejected the traditional measurement system that indicated that 11 percent of the population was in the upper classes and proposed a more convincing four percent. The association of survey agencies (Abipeme Associação Brasileira de Pesquisadores de Mercado) embraced the proposition, but the advertisers' association (ABA - Associação Brasileira de Anunciantes) did not. Thus, for Abipeme, the wealthy Brazilians total less than six million, while ABA and some dissenting survey agencies—including the major ratings institutions IBOPE (Instituto Brasileiro de Opinião Pública e Estatística) and Nielsen—prefer the total of 16 million. The official reason for their dissent was the impossibility of working with smaller statistical proportions for the upper classes (the margin of error would be too large), but observers like Straubhaar point out that the reduction would negatively affect their TV clients (Straubhaar, 1992). The

Brazilian government's survey agency (IBGE - Instituto Brasileiro de Geografia e Estatística), on the other hand, qualified as upper class only those with more than twenty base salaries (which varies with inflation) and includes less than two percent of the population: 2.9 million people. The Brazilian branch of Citbank, interested in working only with clients with monthly incomes above $1500, found an even more restricted market. Its surveys indicated a total of just 1.5 million people in the whole country (1992d).

Since some 44 percent of the population constituted the lower classes D and E (Lima, 1992), it would be natural, for the television industry to emphasize the more popular programming, which is designed to appeal to the lowest common denominator. With only one TV set in a typical household of these social classes, the majority of the audience makes watching television a family activity. The programs must attend to the interests and tastes of a heterogeneous group composed of children, their parents and even grandparents. To fragment the family unit of viewers by tailoring programs to individual tastes collides, therefore, with the fact that the majority of the audience cannot watch television in an individualistic manner—there simply is not another TV set for differing tastes. Only 45 percent of the TV households in Brazil had a second TV set, compared to 65 percent in the United States (Yuster, 1992). Further market segmentation for the lower classes thus seemed to be an impossible task. Contrasted with this was a 1991 study by IBOPE in São Paulo (See table 4 for summary). Results of the study showed that in the richer classes (A, B and C), the average was one person to one TV set, making the consumption of television programming more individualized. In the poorer classes (D and E), the average was four people to one TV set, thus making consumption of television programming typically a family activity.

The same study also revealed that it was only during 55 minutes per day (13 percent of the total time higher-class households dedicated to viewing television) that two or more sets were turned on at the same time; this was more than half the time the second set was on. In only 40 percent of these occasions, 22 minutes, are the sets tuned to different channels. The secondary set represented, therefore, a potential new market for a different kind of programming, one targeted to the more affluent social classes (Lima, 1992).

182

Table 4 - IBOPE survey

Area: Metro Sao Paulo
Sample: 234 households with 1 or more TV sets.
Date: Performed between February 18-March 3, 1991.
Conclusions:
- 90% of households (HH) turn on the TV at least once a day.
- In one week only 2% of HH never turns on the TV and in two weeks the percentage falls to zero.
- 45% of HH with TV sets have more than one set.
- 81% of the sets are color.
- The average time of exposure to TV is seven hours per HH, spread throughout the day in the following manner:

Time of day	Exposure to TV
Between 6 and 12	45 minutes
Between 12 and 6PM	2 hours
Between 6 and 12AM	3h45
After 12AM	30 minutes

- Class is not a significant variable in TV consumption. The number of hours number of hours per day is equal to classes AB, C and DE with variations according to the days of the week.
- The time of exposure to TV is directly connected to the class and age of the housewives, as in the following chart:

Heavy User	AB, young	5.2% of HH belong to this group, which corresponds to 11.3% of sample
Light User	AB, young DE, young	Mostly concentrated on this group

- The children either watch too much or too little, concentrated on the two extremes of the curve.
- The number of TV sets in a HH is considered when defining classes. The sets are divided across classes in the following manner:

Class	Percentage
A, B	67 (more than one set)
C	30
D, E	1

- In the richer classes, the average is one person to one TV set and the consumption is more individualized, while in the poorer classes, the average

183

is four persons to one TV set and the consumption is collective.
• The HHs with more than one TV set (45% of the total) are
exposed seven hours a day on average to television, but only
five hours and a half (78%) are generated by the principal set. The
remaining one hour and a half (22%) is generated by the other sets.
• During only 55 minutes (13% of the total time such HHs
dedicate to TV) two or more sets are turned on at the same
time-and this is, more than half the time the second set is
on. In only 40% of these occasions, 22 minutes, the sets are
tuned to different channels.
• The HBs with VCRs are 33% of the total sample. Their
distribution per class is:

Class	Percentage
A	80
B	60
C	31
D, E	1

• Each BB watches an average of 26 minutes a day (weekdays) of VCR,
corresponding to 5% of the time dedicated to TV. On weekends this
percentage rises to 15% with an average of one hour a day.
• Half of the BBs don't turn on the VCR for one week, but those that do turn
it on more than four days a week.
• Of the TV HHs, 21% has at least one set with remote control. The class
division in this case is:

Class	Percentage
A	71
B	36
C	13

• In the HHs with remote control, the channel is changed each 14 minutes,
which means 4.2 changes per hour. In the HHs without remote control, the
channel is changed three times per hour or once every 20 minutes.

Source: IBOPE

184

In 1982, Walter Clark, widely credited with making TV Globo a success, articulated such market segmentation strategy in raw words: "The dummies that make television in this country have not yet realized that the non-attended public is the class A, capable of sustaining alternative programming, with their high acquisitive power" (Pinto, 1982). The chase for the higher classes and the trade of size for quality audience seemed, indeed, to constitute a new phase of the Brazilian television segmentation, in which the incipient signal distribution technologies came to play an active role. The success of MTV-Abril in attracting large advertisers in spite of the lack of an audience measurement in its first days, and very low ratings confirmed it. At such point, the social class variable assumed two different aspects. One aspect of class is economic capital, the lack or abundance of disposable income, which determines who can afford the expensive new Brazilian pay-television systems. The elitism of these systems was outlined in a Marplan survey of June 1991 among the subscribers of the defunct Canal+. About 504 households out of a total of 20,000 subscribers in São Paulo were contacted over the telephone and their answers clearly denoted a very wealthy group (See table 5). Such a conclusion should come as no surprise, since the American pay-TV also took a very elitist character in the 1970s.The president of CBS network at the time, Arthur R. Taylor, took advantage of that fact to attack the growing competitor:

One in every four American families has an income under $5000 a year; but the best information available to us indicates that only one in eight families that subscribe to cable television has an income below that level. More than one family in every three has an income of $7000; but among families that buy original sports and movies on cable television, only one in nine has an income under $7000. These comparisons suggest that the economic discrimination inherent in pay television has already begun (Taylor, 1975, p.334). Another aspect of class is cultural or educational capital; that is, a group's taste, choice of television content, is largely determined by the educational or cultural attributes of membership in the group. Less obvious than economic capital , cultural capital relies on education and family background to determine who is content or discontent with mass audience programming (Bourdieu, 1984).

185

Table 5 - Marplan survey of STV audience in Brazil

· 89% of the families belong to class A, while the remaining 11% belong to class B.
· 45% of the households earn a monthly family income above $2,500.
· On average, the STV is watched by three persons in each household.
· 53% of the audience is 30+ years old.
· STV is watched more by men (57%) than women (43%).
· 35% of the men are owners or partners in their businesses.
· 25% have positions as directors or managers.
· 32% are liberal professionals, with emphasis in Engineering.
· 59% have completed a university degree.
· 90% use credit cards.
· 71% are members in recreational clubs.
· 56% of the homes have swimming pools.
· 47% have beach homes.
· 36% have country homes.
· 18% have private drivers.
· 10% have a boat or yacht.
· 66% had been in foreign countries (mainly USA nd Europe) in the previous year.
· STV is watched on average 1.7 hours a day during week and 2.3 hours on weekends.

Source: "Jornais fazem campanha para atrair anúncios." Folha de São Paulo, February 11,1991. p.l0.

Even though the elite's dissatisfaction with broadcast television still demands further study and quantification, the willingness of the higher classes to tune to what can be characterized until then as foreign television was certainly greater. Straubhaar's theory of assymetrical interdependence and cultural proximity seems to confirm this statement:

> Upper classes tend to be more internationalized in their tastes, thus more likely to seek and be affected by foreign programs ... than lower middle and lower classes, who more often seem to prefer national broadcast TV programs (Straubhaar, 1991).

And Oliveira goes on to say that:

> Through cable [and any other new system for that matter] there is a direct access to First World programming, which may enhance the already strong identification the rich have with the North. Brazilian elites have adopted [an] international and universal

lifestyle importing massively to sustain international patterns of consumption. From May to October 1990, Brazil imported $595.3 million of superfluous items (Oliveira, 1992).

The relationship between the richer classes and the foreign programming was also determined by a language barrier. Since the majority of foreign programs offered by Brazilian pay-TV were spoken in the original language (or subtitled, which does not help those without fluent reading skills), an expensive foreign-idiom education was necessary to understand the programs. Moreover, the knowledge of a language can be very important in the daily activities of the top jobs held by the higher classes. Illustratively, most of the major English schools in Brazil had started to offer American television programming as a supporting learning tool. First, the schools installed the big satellite dishes to capture AFRTS or CNN, but they later opted to a subscription of UHF/SHF TVA services, which included these channels. In a study about the uses and impact of cable TV in the Dominican Republic, Straubhaar detected the same language gap:

> The reasons for wanting cable TV given by those who have it tend to reveal an instrumental motive, learning English, and a cultural motive, getting access to foreign culture ... the largest group (35%) [of respondents] said it was for their children and the next largest group said it was to learn English (14%). Other reasons were to have greater variety in programming, to see foreign programs, get more information and see more movies (Straubhaar, 1989).

While reasons for subscribing in Brazil were not available for this study, programmers believed that foreign programs in their original sound track would attract some of the largest immigrant groups in the country. The choice for the Italian network RAI's programs within the TVA schedule, for example, was based on the fact that São Paulo houses an Italian community larger than Milan's. Outside Italy, by the way, the Italian-speaking population in South America is larger than in Europe; about 50 percent of Argentine inhabitants come from Italy (Marsiaj, 1990a). PluralSat services, on the other hand, selected programming from the main French channels to attract some of the estimated 200,000 French people living in Brazil (Moreira, 1992). Besides nationality, other variables could be used in the segmentation of the Brazilian television market. The Audience Research Director of IBOPE in São Paulo at the time, Ana Lúcia D'Império Lima, reminds us that many segments of the audience remained unattended or poorly served even then. While there would be no point to an ethnic programming division, she believed that some demographic groups deserved more attention. The children between two and 12 years old, she pointed, were generally treated as one group, while they actually present very diverse behavioristic peculiarities and demand different programming. Between 14 and 19 years old, the teenagers that are eagerly hunted by American television stations had also been neglected in many ways by the Brazilian networks, which apparently assumed that "teenagers didn't watch TV."

An article in Visão magazine suggests that programmers could not be more mistaken. According to IBGE (Instituto Brasileiro de Geografia e Estatística), 30 million of the 155 million inhabitants of Brazil in 1990 were youngsters between 10 and 19 years old, whose main leisure habits were watching television and practicing sports (Vianna, 1990). Further research by MTV-Abril confirmed that this public consisted a very attractive consumer group, consuming for example eight million sneakers and 35 million pairs of jeans every year (Lobo, 1991). The problem, explains Lima from IBOPE, was that segments like MTV's, even though statistically significant in demographic terms (the public within MTV's target age group was 46 percent of the total population), were restricted in social-economic terms. "MTV is directed to the contestant character of teenagers. Their problem is that they usually lack another TV set to protest," she concluded (Lima, 1992). The children, women and the illiterate that supposedly watch more television and would constitute sure target niches for the new segmented television stations in Brazil were, nevertheless, incapable of paying for a more tailored programming.

In the United States, cable networks like Nickelodeon, Lifetime and The Discovery Channel seemed to attend to their respective groups, but in Brazil they could not initially afford to pay a subscription nor even probably consume enough to justify advertising-supported schedules. For the near future, therefore, further segmentation seemed to be restricted to the upper classes and, while the poorer majority of the Brazilians were likely to keep watching the traditional mass networks, a significant drainage of upper class viewers to pay-TV was expected. As soon as the national pay-TV systems were able to insert local commercials in the foreign program schedule, it was inevitable that the advertising investments would also be realigned so as to redirect luxury product spots to the elite pay-TV. Without the elite audience and their advertisers, the low-brow standards, some observers concluded, would become more pervasive.

7
Conclusion

The major purpose of this research was to present an overview of Brazilian developments in the television industry of the early 1990s and to examine the impact of the new television distribution technologies in the growing segmentation of the market—a phenomenon that previously occurred in the United States. From the start, a few hypotheses were made, which demanded confirmation. Initially, it was necessary to prove that the general theories of market segmentation and positioning, as proposed by Kotler, Ries and Trout, could be applied to the television industry. The thesis under test was that television marketing strategies are moving away from a mass target audience, toward more focused targets, whose reduced size is compensated by a higher empathy with the programming and advertising. In the course of this study, the evolution of both American and Brazilian systems have been reviewed through a marketing perspective and many signs of such move were identified as follows.

In the original mass marketing environment, an advertiser controlled television delivered single formula lineups to a very eager and complacent mass of audience. As the novelty of the "radio with images" vanished, however, a more mature audience called in the 1960s for more diversity to attend their rising and diverging expectations. With the support of audience surveys, the product-differentiated environment entered the 1980s with the impossible challenge of offering everything to everybody. New television programming of limited public interest required more channels and transmission time than broadcasters could offer, and new signal distribution technologies came to the rescue. Gradually, the audience was segmented by technology access, programming interests and consumption behavior, provoking a rupture in the mass audience media concept represented by broadcasting television. The dominance of the three large American networks (NBC, CBS and ABC) has declined, as cable networks introduced lineups better suited to specific audience niches. And even though broadcasters still hold the largest share of the advertising investments, cable systems have proved that small audiences can be profitable—as long as advertisers are convinced that this specific audience can be more easily convinced to consume. The whole television business has suffered the impact of thinking small. Stations have increasingly selected shows that attend to audience niches not served by their local competitors, and the break-even ratings have dropped significantly. The American networks have fought the Financial and Syndication Rules to participate more on the lucrative production and syndication side of the industry, while seeking the lost mass audiences at a global level.

A second thesis was based on the premise that Brazilian television tends to follow at a distance the trends experienced by its American counterpart, and therefore should present a similar segmentation trend. The first signs of a segmentation process have been evidenced in the Brazilian television by the decline of Globo TV's quasi-monopoly, and the more frequent attacks from competitor networks targeted at the upper and lower classes. But there is much more to it, as new companies introduced a variety of signal distribution technologies. The two industries were compared to highlight the problems the Brazilian entrepreneurs could expect and to suggest clues for the future of the recently-born companies. Indeed, the resemblance between the industries could be seen in common difficulties, like the lack of UHF receivers, and solutions, such as the option for segmented programming. On the other hand, the Brazilian companies introduced significant adaptations to the American example. While Brazilian cable television was stalled by government policies, just as it happened in the United States, direct broadcast satellite services—which are contemporaneous to cable in Brazil—seemed at the time to have a greater potential in Brazil than in America. However, since most of the new companies have based their operations on the satellite, the better reception for one technology over another may not constitute an issue in Brazil. The new companies are national distributors of imported programming and, with the help of the satellite, can deliver it nationwide to UHF, MMDS or cable systems.

In fact, the Brazilian adaptation of the American television segmentation process is more likely to present a wider variety of technologies competing in the major local markets. While cable's early growth in the U.S. placed it in a position to even block the development of competing technologies, such as it happens with DBS, the contemporaneity of the systems in Brazil assured each one a significant initial segment of the market. The real issues, therefore, were the sources of programming to fill the expanded broadcasting hours suddenly made available and the public demand for the new channels, which would ultimately define the survival of the companies—and the systems. Since there was practically only one company operating within each technology, a company failure could have doomed the system as well, in which case the market could perceive the problem as intrinsic to the technology. Until late 1992, however, most new television channels in the market were enjoying a steady growth, despite the general economic difficulties in Brazil; an exception was made for open UHF TV Jovem Pan, whose owners have abandoned it. Among the pay-TV systems, viability had been associated with the national debate about the real size of the upper classes, a relatively small group in Brazil that is able to pay for extra television leisure. In social terms, these systems have also been criticized for offering imported programming to the elite and increasing the social stratification in a country where the poor majority may be increasingly exposed to a low-brow free TV, while a small rich group enjoy foreign television.

But, as the numerous interviews conducted for this study suggested at the time, the Brazilian scenario was in the midst of a dynamic transition from a tightly controlled television system to one with many more voices. At that point, and with the amount of information made available, it was impossible to predict the feasibility of each system in Brazil. TVA's subscription television was battling GloboSat's DBS in almost every corner of the large metropolitan centers, and this war was just the tip of an iceberg of international interests in the Brazilian market.

According to Ries and Trout, this is the moment of decision, "when future leaders act first and better than competitors." To act better, in this context, may mean avoiding the dependence on foreign lineups and investing in international co-productions—a philosophy mainly practiced by GloboSat and MTV.

Appendix

Currency Exchange

Date	1 dollar is equivalent to
January 8, 1990	NCz$630 (cruzados novos)
October 10, 1990	Cr$92 (cruzeiros)
June 20, 1991	Cr$300.80 (commercial rate)
September 15, 1991	Cr$473

Source: Various newspaper articles. Unless noted, calculation was based on unofficial rates.

References

No-author

Here comes the TV for everybody; ultra high frequency stations, (1951, December) Popular Science, pp. 102-5

Ultra high frequency: the promised land of TV? (1952, August 9) Business Week, pp. 42-3

Ultra high TV in trouble, (1954a, May 29) Business Week, pp. 94

What's happening to UHF? (1954b, October) Consumer Report, pp. 465

Can FCC unscramble fee TV? (1955a, April 2) Business. Week, pp. 40+

Fee TV: why fight's so fierce, (1955b, July 2) Business Week, pp. 27-28

(1955c, November 19). Hopes fade for UHF television. Business Week, p. 27.

(1955d, March 26). Rescuing UHF. Business Week, p. 45-6.

(1955e, October 22). Tryout for new UHF medicine. Business Week, pp, 94.

To pay or not to pay, (1956, March 10) Business Week, pp. 100

Pay-TV controversy gets hotter, (1958, March 1) Business Week, pp. 51

Multiplying users fight for place in radio spectrum, (1959, July 4) Business Week pp. 40-2

At least a viewing for over-the-air pay-TV, (1960, October 22) Business Week, pp. 28-9

TV's $2- million test for UHF, (1961, October 14) Business Week, pp. 115-16

New rush for UHF stations, (1962a, November 3) Business Week, pp. 34+

197

TV trade bends on UHF, (1962b, February 17) Business Week, pp. 40

Will people pay? (1962c, July 16) Business Week pp. 49-50

FCC's bonanza to tuner makers, (1963, July 6) Business Week, pp. 39-40

UHF+VHF= 82, (1964, April 27) Newsweek, pp. 84

Dialing in on UHF, (1966, January 10) Newsweek, pp. 42-3

Television is the message down in Rio, (1967, June 17) Business Week, pp. 86-8

Pay-TV's bad reception, (1968, February 10) Business Week, pp. 23

Os filhos do Direito de Nascer, (1969a, May 7) UHF band strikes-up, (1969b, March 3) Newsweek, pp. 60-1

TV for business; Multipoint distribution service, (1973, July 21) Business Week, pp. 58

Why TV syndicators are striking it rich, (1977, February 28) Business Week, pp. 76+

A questão é ficar atualizado com a tecnologia mundial, (1979a, October 25) Gazeta Mercantil

TV por cabo chega ao Brasil (mas quando?), (1979b, October 28) Jornal do Brasil

How cable TV success hinges on satellites, (1981a, September 14) Business Week, pp. 98-90

Why advertisers are rushing to cable TV, (1981b, November 2) Business Week, pp. 96

Cable programming catches up with demand, (1982a, February 22) Business Week, pp. 130+

Concluído o projeto do serviço de cabo difusão, (1982b, July 28) O Estado de S. Paulo, pp. 9

FCC clears away some underbrush on UHF handicap, (1982c, July 26) Broadcasting pp. 30

O Estado de São Paulo, pp . 14

The rush into cable TV is now turning into a retreat, (1983a, October 17) Business Week, pp. 135+

U.S. cable operators eye a bonanza overseas, (1983b, November 21) Business Week, pp. 112

Viewers turn off subscription TV, (1983c, May 16) Business Week, pp. 28-9

UHF spectrum sharing buried, praised in FCC comments, (1986, July 21) Broadcasting, pp. 36

Dish Owners Speak Out, (1987, September) satellite Orbit, pp. 20-7

Constituição da República Federativa do Brasil (1988) Brasília: Gráfica Oficial do Governo Federal.

Os caminhos do UHF em São Paulo, (1988b, July 4) Meio & Mensagem

Saiu edital para nova TV, (1988c, April 6) Jornal do Brasil

Santo André quer sair na frente com UHF, (1988d, May 14) O Estado de São Paulo

TV par Assinatura: a Globo não quer essa briga, (1988e, May 8) Jornal da Tarde

Brazil's Abril Group (1989a) Abril Group report.

CNN goes Latin via PanamSat, (1989b, January 9) Broadcasting. Encontro decodificado, (1989c, August 26) Jornal da Tarde

Canal+ adiciona publicidade à programação (1990a, January 7) Estado de São Paulo

Canal+ inaugura transmissões em português com campeonato de tênis, (1990b, February 3) Folha de São Paulo

A nova emissora se atrapalha na estréia. Por culpa do computador, (1990c, October 22) Jornal da Tarde

Os planos do canal 21, só de esportes, por Luciano do Vale, (1990d, September 8) Jornal da Tarde

Portaria n° 86 (1990e) Secretaria da Comunicação do Governo Federal. Brasília, DF.

Portaria n º 90 (1990f) Secretaria da Comunicação do Governo Federal. Brasília, DF.

Tem novidade na teve: é o canal 58, (1990g, October 13) Jornal da Tarde

TV Abril vende novo conceito em UHF, (1990h, March 12) Folha da Tarde

Alphaville ganha sua teve. E se aproxima da ficção de Godard, (1991a, January 14) Jornal da Tarde

Até agora, 25 mil assinantes, (1991b, April 29) Meio & Mensagem

Carrossel mexicano, (1991c, June 12) Veja, pp. 78-84

Congresso fica fora de decisão sobre TV a cabo, (1991d, July 2) Jornal do Brasil

A consolidação da MTV e as experiências da Jovem Pan, (1991) (April 29) Meio & Mensagem.

Empresa da 'Raspadinha' quer TV Jovem Pan, (1991f, June 12) Jornal da Tarde

GloboSat abre caminho na TV por assinatura via satélite, (1991g, June 23) O Globo.

Governo prepara regulamentação para TV a cabo, (1991h), November 18) Jornal do Brasil

Juiz veta uso de marca por TV, (1991i, November 7) O Estado de São Paulo

Linha aberta, (1991j, December 11), pp. 88

MTV chega a Porto Alegre, (1991k, October 5) Jornal do Brasil

MTV investe em publicidade, (19911, March 14) Jornal do Brasil

Nike faz campanha exclusiva na MTV, (1991m, July 9) Jornal do Brasil

Nova Emissora, (1991n, June 24) Jornal da Tarde

O canal diferente, (19910, June 19) Veja, pp. 24-

Os amigos na TV, (1991p, June 26) Veja pp. 18-21

A promessa da GloboSat: quatro canais em outubro. Sem esbarrar na lei, (1991q,- September 12) Jornal da Tarde

Radio e TV: o maior poder dos políticos, (1991r, March 11) Jornal da Tarde

Secretaria divulga normas para o serviço de TV a cabo, (1991s, June 11) Gazeta Mercantil

Telas novas em UHF, (1991t, February 13) Veja SP, pp. 16-7

TV a cabo funciona em Franca desde janeiro, (1991u, February 4) Folha de S. Paulo

TV Metropolitana veicula sua primeira campanha, (1991v, March 11) Meio & Mensagem

TV por assinatura inicia sua grande arrancada no mercado, (1991w, May 13) Meio & Mensagem

TV, belo negócio, (1991x, May 31) IstoÉ/Senhor

Um novo hábito, (1991y, October 2) Veja SP, pp. 8-9

Uma nova era, (1991z, October 2) , pp. 100

Cable Television Developments. (1992a) Cable television Advertising Bureau, Inc.

Jornais fazem campanha para atrair anúncios, (1992b, February 11) Folha de São Paulo, pp. 10

O futuro na tela, (1992c, April 8) Veja SP, pp. 26-7

Riqueza se põe na mesa (paid article), (1992d, February 5) Exame, pp. 84-5

Author

Abreu, N. F. d. (1990, August 19). Sumaré vai ganhar quarta antena de TV. O Estado de São Paulo

Alencar, M. (1990, June 11). Brazil launches MTV channel. Hollywood Reporter

Almeida, P. M., & Wickerhauser, H.(1991). Finding a better social economic status classification system for Brazil. (4 - November), 240-50.

Americano, A. C. (1991, September 12). TVA contabiliza 33 mil assinantes. Gazeta Mercantil

Anderaos, R. (1991a, January 27). Jovem Pan copia 'know-how' da CNN e planeja estrear em marco, Folha de São Paulo

Anderaos, R. (1991b, June 3). TVA estréia com dois canais de filmes. Folha de São Paulo, p. 5- 3 .

Andrade, P. (1991, October 16). GloboSat lança TV por assinatura. 0 Globo

Ang, I. (1992). Desperately Seeking the Audience (1st. ed.). London: Routledge.

Annis, D.(TCI's Sales Manager). (1992, December 7). Personal interview. East Lansing, MI.

Apolinário, s. (1991, June 16). Roberto Marinho deu GloboSat para Boni e seu amigo americano. Folha de S. Paulo.

Arruda, G. (1990, June 30). Pan Sat instalará no Sul a primeira televisão a cabo. Gazeta Mercantil.

Arruda, G. (1991, July 24). 90 projetos em montagem.Gazeta Mercantil

Arruda, B. C. (1990). Almanaque Abril (16th. ed.). São Paulo: Editora Abril.

Baldwin, T. F., & McVoy, D. S. (1988). Cable Communications (Second ed.). New Jersey: Prentice Hall.

Barbieri, R. (1985, November/December). STV: R.I.P. Channels Communications, p. 32.

Barnouw, E. (1990). Tube of Plenty: The Evolution of American Television (2nd. ed.). Oxford: Oxford University Press.

Benrey, R. M. (1964, August). ABCs of UHF-TV. Popular Science, p. 104-7.

Bensimon, C. (1991, July 7). TV a cabo promete gerar muita polêmica. Jornal do Brasil.

Blecher, N. (1991, September 13). Televisão muda o perfil do grupo Abril. Folha de S. Paulo.

Boarini, M. (1991, August 7). Cidade decreta o fim do seletor congelado .Folha de São Paulo

Bolano, C. (1988). Mercado Brasileiro de Televisão (1st. ed.). Aracajú: Universidade Federal de Sergipe.

Bourdieu, P. (1984). Distinction: A social critique of the judgement of taste. Cambridge: Harvard University Press.

Bower, R. D. (1973). The Bower Report: Attitudes Toward Broadcasting. In T. C. Smythe & G. A. Mastroianni (Eds.), Issues in Broadcasting (pp. 31-43). Fullerton: Mayfield Publishing Co.

Boyle, J. M. (1980). A Survey of Consumer Attitudes and Experience Regarding UHF Television (Conducted for the Federal Communications Commission No. 792806). Louis Harris and Associates, Inc.

Browne, D. R. (1989). Comparing Broadcasting Systems: the experience of six industrialized nations (1 ed.). Iowa: Iowa State University Press.

Caparelli, S. (1980). Comunicação de Massa Sem Massa. São Paulo: Cortez Editora.

Caparelli, S. (1982,). Televisão e Capitalismo no Brasil. Porto Alegre: L&PM.

Cappia, J. E. (Telecommunications consultant). (1992, January 15). personal interview. São Paulo.

Carla, A. (1991, July 3). Governo pode criar decreto aprovando o uso do sistema já a partir de setembro. Gazeta Mercantil.

Carvalho, J. d. (1991, October 27). GloboSat entra no ar no sábado. O Globo.

Chaim, C. (1991, April 5). IBF poderá adquirir 40% da TV Jovem Pan. Jornal do Brasil

Comodo, R. (1991, July 1). SP terá TV a cabo no ar em setembro. Jornal do Brasil.

Costa, A. H. (1986). Rio e Excelsior: projetos fracassados. In Um País no ar: História da TV Brasileira em três canais (pp. 123-66). São Paulo: Brasiliense.

Costa, L. d. F. (Technical Manager of Jovem Pan). (1992, January 31). Personal interview. São Paulo, SP.

Article with title unknown (1992, January 2) Folha de São Paulo.

Cruz, V. (1991, July 21). Go verno triplica canais de radio e TV para concessão. Folha de S. Paulo

Delmanto, R. (1991, August 29). Teve par assinatura: lances de uma guerra declarada. Jornal da Tarde.

Marketing Department (N.d.) [photocopy of typescript]. Music Television, Rede Abril de Televisão, São Paulo.

Duarte, L. G. (1991). Splitting the Cake (Class Assignment TC 852). Michigan State University. Unpublished.

Duó, E. (1989a, August 11). Dentel acusa irregularidades nas TVs a cabo. Folha de S. Paulo.

Duó, E. (1989b, August 6). Padre opera TV a cabo com canais internacionais no interior de SP. Folha de São Paulo.

Duó, E. (1989c, July 23). SP vai ter sua primeira TV a cabo em condomínio. Folha de São Paulo.

Eastman, S. T. Head, s. W., & Klein, L. (1989). Broadcast/Cable Programming (3rd. ed.). Belmont:Wadsworth Pub. Co.

Fernandes, E. L. (1990, March). No ar, novos campeões de audiência. Revista Nacional de Telemática, p. 25-32.

Fernandes, I. (1982). Memória da Telenovela Brasileira. São Paulo: Proposta Editorial.

Filho, H. A. (1976). O ópio do povo: O sonho. e a Realidade. São Paulo: Símbolo.

Flesch, J. N. (1990, November 20). MTV altera programação depois de um mês no ar. Folha da Tarde.

Foster, E. S. (1982). Understanding Broadcasting (2nd. ed.). Addison-Wesley. França, L. (1991, April 25). Regulamentação permitirá a venda de espaço. Gazeta Mercantil.

Furtado, R. (1988). Programação I: Da Rede Tupi à Rede Manchete, uma visão histórica. In TV ao Vivo:

Depoimentos (pp. 57-69). São Paulo: Brasiliense.

Gancia, B. (1990, January 24). Novo canal traz programação da RAI, CNN e TV-M. O Estado de São Paulo.

Gaspar, M. (1991, March 17). A jovem MTV, fazendo a cabeça das gravadoras. Jornal da Tarde.

Giannini, S. (1989, March, 1). Canal UHF da Jovem Pan aposta na fórmula ágil do rádio. Folha de S. Paulo.

Goldstein, S. (1984, November/December). STV: downhill racer. Channels Communications.p , 42.

Graciosa, H. M. M.(CPqD engineer). (1988, July). Personal Interview. Campinas, SP.

Grover, R. (1987, April 6). Fox's new network goes after the baby boomers. Business Week p. 41+.

Grover, R., & Liberman, D. (1989, January 9). In the race for viewers, the networks fall further behind. Business Week, p. 80-1.

Head, S. W., & Sterling, C. H. (1990). Broadcasting in America (Sixth ed.). Boston: Houghton Mifflin Co.

Hertzberg, R. (1954, January). TV's seventy new channels. Popular Science, p. 177-82.

Hoineff, N. (1991). TV em expansão (1st. ed ,) , São Paulo: Record.

Iori, C. (1992, May 12). TVA e Globosat brigam por assinaturas. Folha de São Paulo, p. 4-5.

Jaffe, D. L. (1974). Cable Communications: Up from CATV. In T.C. Smythe & G. A. Mastroianni (Eds.), Issues in Broadcasting (pp. 280-9). Fullerton: Mayfield Publishing

Jones, T. (General Manager of ABC Affiliate). (1992, July). Personal interview. Lansing, MI.

Kamakura, W. A., & Mazzon, J. A. (1991). Value segmentation: a model for the measurement of values and value system. 18 (September), 208-18.

205

Kotler, P. (1986). Principles of Marketing (3rd. ed i), Englewood Cliffs: Prentice Hall.

Lachtermacher, S. (1991, April 9). O computador comanda a MTV. Jornal do Brasil.

Lazaretti, M. (1992, MTV, em paz com seu público). Jornal da Tarde.

LEDA (1983). Investimento Publicitário: Verba e Participação. In 1º semestre de 82 a 1º semestre de 83

Lima, A. L. (Audience Research Director of IBOPE São Paulo). Personal interview (1992, January 29).

Litman, B. (1991). Economics of the Mass Media. Manuscript for TC852, Michigan State University.

Lobo, T. (1991, August 12). MTV inova e fatura US$ 10 milhões em 91. Jornal do Brasil.

Luiz, A. (1989, June 12). Grupo de Mídia discute o UHF no Brasil e no mundo. Meio & Mensagem.

Luz, S. R. (1992, May 6). Acerto fora do ar. Veja SP, p. 10-1.

MacGregor, J. (1973). Pay-TV May Hold Key to Cable-TV's Future. In T. C. Smythe & G. A.Mastroianni (Eds.), Issues in Broadcasting (pp. 323-30). Fullerton: Mayfield Publishing Co.

Magalhães, T. (1991, October 12). TVA e Globosat: a guerra por trás das telas. Jornal da Tarde.

Mageste, P. (1989, July 15). Canal+ vai investir em jornalismo. Folha da Tarde.

Magyar, V. (19B9, March 29). Mais uma emissora no ar. Em UHF. Jornal da Tarde.

Maiello, C. (1988, February 5). A Jovem Pan inaugura o UHF. Jornal da Tarde.

Mann, M. (1950, August). How your town could get big-city TV. Popular Science, p , 111-4.

Marques, T. (1991, January 28). Comercialização da MTV supera expectativas. Meio & Mensagem.

Marsiaj, A. (1990a, January 23). São Paulo ganha mais três canais par assinatura. Folha de São Paulo.

Marsiaj, A. (1990b, January 4). SP terá cinco TVs em UHF ainda este ano. Folha de São Paulo.

Martinho, M. E. (1990, June 10). MTV poderá ser captada via satélite fora de SP. Folha de S.Paulo.

Mattos, S. A. S. (1990). Um perfil da TV Brasileira (40 anos de história: 1950-1990) (1st. ed.). Salvador: Associação Brasileira de Agências de Propaganda.

Mauad, I. e., & Rocha Filho, M. F. d. (1990, January 8). A TV para quem sabe o que quer. O Globo.

Mawakdye, A. (1992, February 2). Antenas. Uma perigosa forma de poluição. Shopping News.

Melo, J. M. (1985). Comunicação e Transição Democrática. Porto Alegre: Mercado Aberto.

Melo, J. M. (1988·). As telenovelas da Globo: Produção e Exportação. São Paulo: Summus.

Melo, J. M. d. (1992). Brazil's role as a television exporter within the Latin American regional market. In ICA, (pp.1-14). Miami: FL.

Mesquita, H. (1982). Tupi: A greve da fome. São Paulo: Cortez Editora.

Mink, E. (1983, December). Why the networks will survive cable. Atlantic, p. 63-6+.

Monteiro, N. (1991a, March 15). TV a cabo em alguns bairros de Curitiba. Gazeta Mercantil.

Monteiro, N. (1991b, July 26). TVA chega a Curitiba em outubro.

Monush, B. (1992) .Television & Video Almanac 1992 (37th. ed.). New York: Quigley Publishing Co.

Moreira, V. (1992, January 13). Emissoras por assinatura esquentam as turbinas. O Estado de São Paulo, p. 5.

Nery, M. (1991, August 14). No trono doméstico.Veja, p. 1002.

Netto, R. S. (1990, August). A tela do rock. Imprensa, p. 367.

Nicolau, R. (1991, April 9). Minas inaugura TV a cabo. Jornal do Brasil.

Nogueira, L. (1988). Telejornalismo I: A experiência da Rede Globo. In C. Macedo, A. Falcão, & C. J. M. Almeida (Eds.), TV ao Vivo: Depoimentos (pp. 81-92). São Paulo: Brasiliense.

Nunes, N. (1987, December 20). A Jovem Pan (não) é só rádio! Gazeta Esportiva.

Oliveira, O. S. (1992). High Tech Allienation in Brazil. In International Communications Associatior (ICA), (pp.18). Miami: FL

Park, R. E. (1970). Potencial Impact of Cable Growth on Television Broadcasting No. R-587-FF). The Rand Corporation.

Picillo, G. (1989, March 7). Articulação dos novos canais. Gazeta Mercantil.

Pimenta, A. (1990, February 4). As ondas UHF invadem o céu de São Paulo. O Estado de S. Paulo , p. 45.

Pinto, J. N. (1982, August 1). TV paga no Brasil será UHF codificado . Jornal do Brasil, p. 4.

Regina, A. (1990, March 12). Abril promete revolução na televisão brasileira. Meio & Mensagem.

Ries, A., & Trout, J. (1981). Positioning: The Battle for Your Mind (1st ed.). New York: McGraW-Hill.

Ries, A., & Trout, J. (1987). Marketing of War (1st. ed.). São Paulo: McGraW-Hill.

Rito, R. (1991a, June 12). TV de elite. Jornal do Brasil.

Rita, R. (1991b, October 12). TV por satélite terá até novela. Jornal do Brasil.

Rodrigues, A. (1991, June 10). TVA chega ao Rio em agosto. Jornal do Brasil.

Sá, N. d. (1990, January 7). Sarney espera recesso e distribui mais 10 TVs. Folha de S. Paulo.

Sá, N. d. (1991, November 3). MTV completa um ano no Brasil e quer virar a Record dos anos 90. Folha de São Paulo. TVA saleswoman. (1992, January 31). Personal interview. São Paulo, SP.

Sampaio, M. F. (1984). História do Rádio e da TV no Brasil e no Mundo. Rio de Janeiro: Achiame/Vozes.

Sanoff, A. P. (1985, September 23). TV tries to sharpen focus on its viewers. U.S. News World Republic, p. 60.

Santomauro, A. (1991, August 26). TVA conquista seus primeiros anunciantes. Meio & Mensagem.

Sastre, v. (1991, June 13). "GloboSat" promete superar padrão global. O Estado de s. Paulo.

Sayão, F. (1990, October 17). Abril estréia no sábado TV dirigida só para os jovens. Gazeta Mercantil.

Schiffman, L. G., & Kanuk, L. L. (1991). Consumer Behavior (Fourth ed.). New York City: Prentice Hall.

Schramm, W., & Alexander, J. (1973). Survey of Broadcasting: Structure, Control, Audience. In T. C.

Smythe & G. A. Mastroianni (Eds.), Issues in Broadcasting (pp. 8-31). Fullerton: Mayfield Publishing Co.

Schwartsman, A. (1991a, January 20). Emissora só de filmes chega ao Brasil com um acervo de cinco mil títulos. Folha de São Paulo.

Schwartsman, A. (1991b, September 15). TVA entra no ar ao meio-dia de hoje. Folha de São Paulo, p.6-3.

Serapicos, M. (1991, February 11). Novos canais nas telas brasileiras. Sem novelas. Jornal da Tarde.

Serapicos, M. & Sastre, V. (1991, June 13). TVA e GloboSat, duelo antes da hora. Jornal da .Tarde.

Silva, A. (1991, June 17). Começa a guerra das TVs por assinatura . Meio & Mensagem.

Silva, F. d. B. e. (1990, August 19). Abril se associa à TV Corcovado e inicia rede. Folha de São Paulo.

Silva, L. E. P. C. (1982). Estratégia empresarial e estrutura organizacional nas emissoras de televisão brasileiras (1950 a 1982). São Paulo: EASP/FGV, mimeo.

Silva, R. A. V. (GloboSat São Paulo Sales Manager). (1992, January 22). Personal interview. São Paulo, SP.

Sodré, M. (1981). O monopólio da Fala. Petrópolis: Vozes.

Straubhaar, J. D. (1989). The uses and effects of cable in the Dominican Republic. In International Communication Association.

Straubhaar, J. D. (1991). Beyond Media Imperialism: Asymmetrical Interdependence and Cultural proximity. [Typescript photocopy], 8, 1-11.

Straubhaar, J. D. (personal Communication to author). (1992, December 4).

Taylor, A. R. (1975). Does the American family need another mouth to feed? In T. C. Smythe & G. A. Mastroianni (Eds.), Issues in Broadcasting (pp. 330-2). Fullerton: Mayfield Publishing Co.

Teixeira, A. (1988, August 29). Grupo Abril vence a disputa pela concessão. Gazeta Mercantil.

Teixeira, F. (1991, January 8). Nova programação da MTV vai até 3h. Folha da Tarde.

Tepfer, C. (1962, October). More TV channels for everyone: UHF as well as VHF. Popular Science, p. 125-7+.

Tessman, B. (Fox Affiliate Chief Engineer). (1992, May 17). Personal interview. Lansing, MI.

Vampré, O. A. (1979). Raízes.e Evolução do Rádio e da Televisão. Porto Alegre: FEPLAM/RBS.

Varis, T. (1974). Global Traffic in Television. In T. C. Smythe & G. A. Mastroianni (Eds.), Issues in Broadcasting (pp. 372-80). Fullerton: Mayfield Publishing Co.

Vianna, I. S. (1990, September 5). Ainda sem falar o dialeto jovem. Visão, p , 58-61.

Vizia, G. d. (1990, October 10). As ondas exclusivas. O Globo.

Webb, C. (Ann Arbor HSC Affiliate President). Personal interview (1992, May 19).

Xavier Filho, S. (1991, June 26). Boni da Bandeirantes. IstoÉ/Senhor, p, 44-6.

Xexéo, A. (1990, October 23). Faltou som na estréia da MTV. Jornal do Brasil.

Yuster, L. C. (1992). Broadcasting & Cable Market Place 1992. New Providence, NJ: R.R. Bowker.

Zoglin, R. (1990, November 19). Goodbye to the mass audience. Time, p. 122-3.

www.ingramcontent.com/pod-product-compliance
Lightning Source LLC
Chambersburg PA
CBHW070107290526
45789CB00005B/1959